Unlocking Spiritual Seeing

Removing the Blockages to Spiritual Sight

by

Dr. Ron M. Horner

Unlocking Spiritual Seeing

Removing the Blockages to Spiritual Sight

By

Dr. Ron M. Horner

PO Box 2167
Albemarle, North Carolina 28002
www.CourtsOfHeaven.Net

Unlocking Spiritual Seeing

Removing the Blockages to Spiritual Sight

Copyright © 2019 Dr. Ron M. Horner

Scripture is taken from the New King James Version®. Copyright © 1982 by Thomas Nelson. Used by permission. All rights reserved. (Unless otherwise noted.)

Scripture quotations are taken from the Amplified® Bible (AMP), Copyright © 1954, 1958, 1962, 1964, 1965, 1987 by The Lockman Foundation.

Scripture quotations marked (TPT) are from The Passion Translation®, Copyright © 2017, 2018 by BroadStreet Publishing Group, LLC. Used by permission. All rights reserved. ThePassionTranslation.com

All rights reserved. This book is protected by the copyright laws of the United States of America. This book may not be copied or reprinted for commercial gain or profit. The use of short quotations or occasional page copying for personal or group study is permitted and encouraged. Permission will be granted upon request.

Requests for bulk sales discounts, editorial permissions, or other information should be addressed to:

LifeSpring Publishing
PO Box 2167
Albemarle, NC 28002 USA

Additional copies available at www.courtsofheaven.net

ISBN 13 TP: 978-0-359-85859-0
ISBN 13 eBook: 978-0-359-88865-8

Cover Design by Darian Horner Design
(www.darianhorner.com)
Image: 123rf.com # 32756196

First Edition: October 2019

10 9 8 7 6 5 4 3 2 1

Printed in the United States of America

Table of Contents

Acknowledgments i
Foreword iii
Preface v
Chapter 1 Unlocking Spiritual Seeing 1
Chapter 2 Opening Blinded Eyes 13
Chapter 3 The Promise of Seeing 19
Chapter 4 Obstacles to Seeing – Part 1 27
Chapter 5 Obstacles to Seeing – Part 2 35
Chapter 6 Obstacles to Seeing – Part 3 41
Chapter 7 Obstacles to Seeing– Part 4 47
Chapter 8 Obstacles to Seeing – Part 5 53
Chapter 9 The Observer Effect 65
Chapter 10 In Conclusion 75
Appendix A I
Accessing the Realms of Heaven I
Courts Mentioned VII
Process Charts IX
Description XLI
Works Cited XLIII
Book Summary XLV

Acknowledgments

Natalie Olson & Jennifer Jones were the instruments God used to unlock insight into some of the concepts disclosed in this book. Now multitudes are unlocking their ability to see in the realm of the spirit. It is an exciting journey. Thank you ladies.

Foreword

I am delighted to write this foreword regarding *Unlocking Spiritual Seeing*, not only because Dr. Ron Horner has been a friend and colleague for quite some time now, but also because I believe deeply in his educative revelation and interpretive insight that he shares with believer's around the world.

I also know that believers at every level and stage of their walk with God can enrich and strengthen their seeing abilities by learning the discussion-driven patterns and practices presented in this book. I can personally speak and say that as an author Dr. Horner is cutting-edge from his books such as *Engaging the Mercy Court of Heaven,* to *Overturning the False Verdicts of Freemasonry* his revelation is biblically sound. Out of the many voices heard in this hour Dr. Horner is a trusted one.

A quote from the book: *"A lot of people do not realize that they made a covenant with their eyes, or that their ancestors did then they got involved in Freemasonry and it's impacting their ability to see in the here and now. It may have been two, three, four, five generations (or more) back in their lineage".*

How many times have you asked yourself why? Concerning any area in your spiritual life where it didn't line-up or it simply didn't make sense. Dr. Horner's *Unlocking Spiritual Seeing* is a tool. If applied, it can bring immediate results and fruit in the life of the challenged believer, thus empowering them as a "Spiritual Life Champion"

Sincerely yours,

Brian L. Johnson

Preface

As we neared the end of a session in the Courts of Heaven a thought came to me. The two ladies I had been working with were able to see our activity in the Courts in a limited way. They recognized that there was a ceiling on their ability to see more extensively and with greater detail. Both had already dealt with the Freemasonry interference in their seeing ability, but neither had even considered the next step we were about to take.

Holy Spirit indicated that we were looking at an ownership issue. Something from their past had laid a spiritual claim upon their ability to see, and that claim had impeded their ability to see for decades. It was time for freedom to come!

As we went through the process, I immediately had each of them test it. We revisited the document we had seen in the courts earlier. Whereas both had been able to see the headlines on the page of the document, none had been able to read the text on the page—until now. They both could read the text on the scrolls they were seeing! It was instantaneous and liberating!

Over the next few months, I followed the same pattern over and over with similar results. Nearly everyone with whom I worked was able to see in the realm of the spirit. As believers helping people see spiritually, we need to be able to visualize the realm of Heaven so we can cooperate with the instructions coming to us from Heaven. It is a vital part of our walk.

As we progressed in understanding, we found a few more keys to help unlock the balance of individuals with whom the initial keys were not successful. The rate of success has increased. We believe as you work through this book, your ability to perceive and see will be completely unlocked. May you be able to freely say, *"Blessed are the pure in heart for they SHALL see God!"* (Matthew 5:8)

When ministering to people, regardless of where they are from on the planet, many suffer from the same issues. One of the predominant situations I deal with is the inability of people to see in the realm of the spirit or to be able to hear God's voice. As we have continued in helping people work in the Courts of Heaven, we have found some helpful keys.

As a result, we have had strong success in helping people be able to see spiritually. In many cases, it happens instantaneously. It is not uncommon for us to work through the steps listed in subsequent chapters of this book and observe instant freedom in people. Invariably they will begin to describe (usually in detail) what they see of Heaven. As I coach them through what they are seeing and how to look a little more intently, they don't even realize that they ARE seeing!

One lady I worked with saw Jesus beside her and a river in front of her. I invited her to jump into the river with Jesus. She commented that she could not swim, but I encouraged her that the rules in Heaven are quite different from those on the earth. She jumped in and realized she could breathe underwater. She had no fear!

I asked if she saw the fish and her comment, "Yes, I've never seen a pink fish!" God has infinite variety in the realms of Heaven.

Jesus unveiled a secret when he told us we must become as a little child to enter the Kingdom of Heaven.

> *Assuredly, I say to you, whoever does not receive the kingdom of God as a little child will by no means enter it. (Mark 10:15)*

As you read this book, I challenge you to be a kid again. Allow Holy Spirit to unlock your (leave out "for you") ability to see in the realm of the spirit. It is available, and you CAN do it! You CAN see! It's not just for other people! We may not all be "seers," but we all can be "seeing!"

Author's Note

Process Charts have been created from many of the steps described in the book. These will be found in the Appendix.

Chapter 1
Unlocking Spiritual Seeing

Do you have trouble seeing or hearing in the realm of the Spirit? If you do, I have some solutions for you, one that we've recently discovered that we have excellent results from, and that will help you unlock your spiritual seeing or hearing.

The Freemasonry Connection

I have found in about 90% of the time when people tell me that they are having trouble seeing or hearing in the spirit, it has a direct connection to Freemasonry oath that was taken by them or one of their ancestors.

In one of the books that I wrote, called *Overcoming the False Verdicts of Freemasonry*, I point out that one of the first things that you do when you become a Freemason is you take an oath to be spiritually blind. They don't call it that, of course, but by allowing the blindfold they call the hoodwink over your eyes, you are, in essence, taking an oath to become spiritually blind and only be able to see the darkness that they put forth as truth. You exchange light for darkness, thinking the darkness is light.

A lot of people do not realize that they made that covenant with their eyes, or that their ancestors did when they got involved in Freemasonry and it's impacting their ability to see in the here and now. It may have been two, three, four, five generations (or more) back in their lineage. A consequence of the oaths of Freemasonry is they tie the person, their immediate family, and ALL future generations to the demon gods of Freemasonry. Regardless of whether you know of any Freemasonry in your lineage because the allegiances your ancestors swore were to various demon gods, you can still be experiencing impact.

A friend, of Mexican descent, has no Freemasonry in his lineage. However, every time he goes through my book on Freemasonry, he gets more and more deliverance. In his bloodlines, ancestors made swore oaths and made covenants with some of the same demonic entities. If you are of European descent, the likelihood that you have Freemasonry in your lineage is very strong. If you had ancestors who were slaves, the likelihood that the masters who owned your ancestors were Freemasons is strong as well.

Freemasonry has tried to infect everyone in some fashion. If you ever bought a meal from a Shriner's Fish Fry, Satan considers it a condoning of Freemasonry and spiritually ties you to Freemasonry and its wickedness.

Some people say, well, I can't be affected by what my grandfather did. Well, you certainly are, you have genetic characteristics and physical characteristics that your grandparents had, that your parents had, that others had in your lineage. Why you can't have that in the spirit?

In the realm of the Spirit, we have many things that we've inherited that we had nothing to do with personally. In Psalm 7, David asks the question, "What is this judgment that I am enjoined to?" He realized that he was dealing with a false judgment against his life that he was not the one which originally received a false judgment. One of his ancestors had that false judgment, and it was causing him trouble in his life today. Sometimes that's the case in your situation.

Spiritual Liens

The second discovery made in helping people unlock their spiritual seeing involves the concept of spiritual liens. Getting the lien removed from your spiritual seeing, is a very new understanding that we came into recently. Every time we have used it, we have had dramatic results. People can see that had not been able to see clearly before or even see at all.

I'm excited to bring this word to you because it's going to help you and help some of your friends and family members be able to see in the realm of the spirit.

We deal with these in the Court of Heaven known as the Court of Titles and Deeds. In this court, we find that people have false titles against their life, or liens against their life, or false notes against their life, or even false lease agreements against their life.

In Psalm 24:7, it says,

The earth is the Lord's, and the fullness thereof, the world and all that dwell therein.

You and I are the property of the Lord of Hosts. However, the enemy realizes that most believers do not understand this concept, so he tries to use his power and get false titles or liens against us.

Sometimes people do those same kinds of things; particularly if they are influential in our life (parents, grandparents, siblings, pastors, teachers, etc.). One arena that they have to influence is in our spiritual seeing.

Recently, I was working with a couple of ladies. One of the ladies, when she was younger, she had heard it said over her, "Oh, you won't be able to hear, or see in the spirit." Because the person speaking was a great authority over her life – her grandmother; it had a great impact — more than she realized. She then found that she was having trouble seeing or hearing in the spirit.

We accessed the Court of Titles and Deeds and found that she had a lien against her spiritual seeing. This lien essentially placed a block on her spiritual seeing. We got that lien released and satisfied by the blood of Jesus, and immediately, her sight was dramatically improved. Where she had only been able to see blurry images, she was able to read the words and documents that she saw in the realm of the Spirit.

With one of the ladies, it was her grandmother who had said to her, "Oh, you won't be able to see," so subsequently, she had trouble seeing. When we stepped into the Court of Titles and Deeds, we asked the question, "Is there a spiritual lien against her seeing?" We asked the question and immediately got the answer, "Yes!" The woman immediately had a sense of who the person responsible for the spiritual lien was. She saw the event where that had occurred in her life, so we then forgave her grandmother for what she had said, we blessed her, and we released her. In John 20:23, Jesus told us, whoever sins, we forgive--are forgiven and whoever sins, we retain--are retained to them. I will choose to forgive someone, as opposed to retaining their sin, because I want my sins forgiven as well.

Let me first explain what a lien is. If you were a homeowner and you hired a roofer to repair your roof. He comes and finishes the job, but you refused to pay him. He would be entitled to get a Mechanic's Lien (or Workman's Lien) against your property. That means that if you attempt to sell your house, you would be required to satisfy that debt before selling the house. The enemy has enticed people to place spiritual liens upon us at times, which slows down our forward progress. Now, let's continue.

Open Heavens

In John Chapter 10, Jesus said, "My sheep know My voice, and they follow Me." We cannot follow Jesus without knowing His voice. If we can hear Him, we should also be able to see Him.

In Matthew 3, when Jesus came up out of the water and said immediately, the heavens were opened, and they heard a voice, and they saw a dove. When the heavens are opened over your life, seeing and hearing should be unveiled to you -- be unlocked to you.

One of the things about unlocking sight is what happens when people make a spiritual lien upon your seeing, or your hearing is that it is almost like they were putting a tarp, or tarpaulin over you and covering so that you can't see through of that tarp.

If you can imagine you're sitting there in your living room and somebody has laid a large tarp or a large blanket over you. You won't be able to see through that blanket, or through that tarp, to see the things that you need to see. In the realm of the spirit, that is what happens to us. When they get this lien upon us, it is like they put a tarp over our seeing or our hearing, and it hinders us from seeing or hearing clearly.

Now again, what we did with the young lady was:

- We forgave her grandmother,
- We blessed her, and
- We released her.

- We asked that that lien against her spiritual sight and hearing be marked satisfied by the blood of Jesus. And finally,
- We requested that the tarpaulin be removed from her life so that she could see and hear in the realm of the spirit.

Once we had done that, we felt a release in our spirit. The Judge had granted our request. I then asked her to check it out--let's see something; let's look at something that you had trouble seeing.

We had just a few moments before completed a court case for someone else, and she was one of the assistants in that court case. She had a little trouble seeing some of the things that we were looking into, so we looked again at those things, and she was able to see what she had not been able to see before.

The other lady that we were working with at the same time also had a lien against her spiritual seeing. It came from another individual in her past, and when we asked the question, "Is there a lien against my spiritual seeing?" Immediately she had an image of this event that had occurred years and years before that had shut down her seeing. This situation also involved someone in a position of authority, speaking a lien over the lady.

Again, we chose to forgive the person for saying what they did, and for creating that lien against her life. We blessed that person, and we released them, from the bondage that the sin had held upon their life. We requested that the lien be satisfied by the blood of Jesus and the tarpaulin to be removed.

Again, we felt a release in our spirit, and we said, okay, let's check this out. We stepped back into where we had been in a court case where we were reading a medical record concerning someone, and she immediately could begin to read clearly what she only could see bits and pieces of, prior just a few minutes before.

We have seen this concept work over and over – often with dramatic, immediate results. We believe the same thing can happen to you.

Shutting Down our Seeing

The third reason that I find that people have trouble seeing or hearing is that they saw something in the spirit realm that scared them. They may have been very young, and out of that fear, they chose to shut down the ability to see or hear. They may have said something like, "I don't want to see anything anymore, that was too scary for me!" Anytime we cooperate with fear; it can lock us down spiritually.

As a result, the person's ability to see in the spirit (or even use their imagination) has been shut down or at least seriously curtailed. Dr. Mark Virkler founder of Christian Leadership University and Communion with God Ministries teaches that we can change the pictures in the mind simply by inviting Jesus into them. By working through imagery, trauma can be released, and emotions can heal. (Tolman, 2017, p. 114)

Following that idea, we have the person recall the last time they could see in the spirit, imagine, or visualize --- particularly the situation where they shut down their seeing ability. Once they see it in their imagination, we ask them to invite Jesus into the scene with them. When he shows up, the fear that they had been experiencing simply dissipates – it's gone!

We then have them repent for shutting down their seeing capabilities and forgive anyone who played a part in that event. We have them bless the person (or persons) and release them. We then ask the Just Judge to restore our ability to see spiritually.

Once these things are complete, we have the person begin to tell us what they are seeing. I ask them to give us a tour of where they are and what they are observing. Invariably, they begin to describe in detail the colors, sights, and even the sounds of what they are visualizing. They often do not even realize they see again until we point it out to them.

Steps to Unlocking Seeing

- Recall the last time you could see clearly
- Invite Jesus into the scene
- Let the fear dissipate
- Repent for shutting down the imagination and for embracing fear

- Forgive anyone who played a part
- Bless them
- Release them
- Ask the Just Judge to restore the sight
- Practice seeing

We have discovered a few other things along the way, but the ones presented thus far are the predominant ones. As you go through the exercises, immediately test out your seeing ability. Understand that some of our seeing is a matter of stewardship, meaning that as we steward the little we do see, we will receive more.

Jesus said this about hearing:

> *[24] Then He said to them, "Take heed what you hear. With the same measure you use, it will be measured to you; and to you who hear, more will be given. [25] For whoever has, to him more will be given; but whoever does not have, even what he has will be taken away from him." (Mark 4:24-25)*

I believe the same principle applies to seeing.

If all you see are some scattered lights in a field of darkness, focus on the lights. What you focus on becomes clearer and larger.

The Prophet Ezekiel had a practice that we can learn from today. He would choose to *look*, and then he would *behold!* The word look means "to see, to gaze upon, to perceive (as a vision), to view.[1] The word *behold* meant "to see" [2] Because Ezekiel would choose to look, he would be enabled to see.

> *By choosing to look, I am being empowered to see!*

If you will notice in reading the book of Ezekiel, he was able to engage the same vision over and over. Every time he went to the valley by the River Chebar, he would step into a vision. Every time he stepped into the vision; he would see something new—something he had not noticed before. Not unlike if I were to visit your home and on the first visit, I would notice things, but the next time I visited your home, I would notice things that were not apparent to me before. Ezekiel shows us that we can revisit a vision.

Job refers to a dream as a night vision [3], and I believe (and this has been my experience) that we can revisit dreams or visions as needed to gain the full message of the dream of vision. We all have had dreams that we promptly forgot upon waking, or we knew God was speaking, but we missed some of the details. We can step back into that vision or dream and ask him to show us what else we need to see. The insight to revisit dreams or

---

[1] Strong, H7200.
[2] Strong, H2009
[3] Job 33:15

visions has been a helpful tool in maximizing dreams and visions.

Chapter 2
Opening Blinded Eyes

When ministering to people, regardless of where they are from on the planet, many suffer from the same issues. One of the predominant situations I deal with is the inability of people to see in the realm of the spirit or to be able to hear God's voice. As we have continued in helping people work in the Courts of Heaven, we have found some helpful keys.

As a result, we have had strong success in helping people be able to see spiritually. In many cases, it happens instantaneously. It is not uncommon for us to work through the things we will talk about in a few minutes, and I will ask the person to close their eyes and tell me what they are seeing or sensing. Invariably they will begin to describe (usually in detail) what they see of Heaven. As I coach them through what they are seeing and how to look a little more intently, they don't even realize that they ARE seeing!

One lady, having seen a river, I invited to jump in the river with Jesus, who was standing beside her. She commented that she could not swim, but I encouraged her that the rules in Heaven are quite different from those on the earth. She jumped in and realized she could breathe underwater. She had no fear!

I asked if she saw the fish and her comment, "Yes, I've never seen a pink fish!" God has infinite variety in the realms of Heaven.

Jesus unveiled a secret when he told us we must become as a little child to enter the Kingdom of Heaven.

> *Assuredly, I say to you, whoever does not receive the kingdom of God as a little child will by no means enter it. (Mark 10:15)*

As you read this book, I give you permission to not be an adult for a little while. Allow Holy Spirit to unlock for you your ability to see in the realm of the spirit. It is available, and you CAN do it! You CAN see! It's not just for other people! We may not all be "seers," but we all can be "seeing!"

The body of Christ has been guilty of dismissing anything that has been hijacked by others. The understanding of how spiritual seeing works is one of those things stolen. We must realize you never copy something that has no value. Our responsibility – learn to use it correctly

> *Remember, what you honor you will have the benefit of.*

If I honor the ability to see, I will be enabled to see. If I honor visions, dreams, etc., I will be enabled to experience them.

Paul tells us that "we have the mind of Christ," [4] and if we have the mind of Christ, then we have access to His thoughts, His mindsets, His way of doing things because we are IN Him. We are not apart from Him. We joined in union with Him.

> *But he who is joined to the Lord is one spirit with Him. (1 Corinthians 6:17)*

The imagery used in that passage is of husband and wife in intimacy with one another – they are one flesh. We are one spirit with Jesus Christ. We are welded together.

Some of us have entertained fear that we will, instead of seeing from Heaven's realm, we will see some demon or something of that sort. I have a promise, however:

> *[7] "Ask, and the gift is yours. **Seek**, and you'll discover. Knock, and the door will be opened for you. [8] For every persistent one will get what he asks for. **Every persistent seeker** will discover*

---

[4] 1 Corinthians 2:16

what he longs for. And everyone who knocks persistently will one day find an open door.

⁹ "Do you know of any parent who would give his hungry child, who asked for food, a plate of rocks instead? ¹⁰ Or when asked for a piece of fish, what parent would offer his child a snake instead? ¹¹ If you, imperfect as you are, know how to lovingly take care of your children and give them what's best, **how much more ready is your heavenly Father to give wonderful gifts to those who ask him?"** *(Matthew 7:7-11) (TPT) (Emphasis mine)*

I'm not asking demons; I'm not inviting them to the party! I am asking of my heavenly Father who has good things for me and wants me to know His will. I am engaging Heaven – not hell. I refuse to be terrorized by unwelcome guests – you can too! Refuse anything but the truth!

Sometimes people tell me, all I see is darkness. We forget, however, that God created the darkness. It was part of the creative work that He called good. If all you're seeing is darkness, look a little deeper. Look a little longer. Focus on the light you do see! It will increase. You don't have to fear darkness. We often are too focused on darkness and not focused enough on light.

If we are not able to see in the spirit, let's find out the legal reason that the seeing is shut down. Typically, it falls into just a few simple categories. We have talked about some of these already, but here is a longer list:

- Masonic covenants
- Covenants or vows we made not to see
- Ownership claims on our sight
- Wrong beliefs about seeing and imagination

The basic premise of the Courts of Heaven paradigm can summarized this way:

---
*If your prayer is unanswered,
we can find out a legal reason why.*

When the legal obstacle(s) to your prayer being answered are dealt with successfully, the answers will come!

It is the same when it comes to being able to see. We need to uncover the obstacle (or obstacles), so the answer can come.

When I am ministering deliverance, I will seek to uncover the legal reason why the demon had entered into the persons' life. Once that reason is discovered and dealt with – usually through repentance and or forgiveness, I don't have to cast out the demon. It simply has no legal right to stay and must vacate the premises. Deliverance is so much easier in the Courts of Heaven! Yay! No more screaming at demons! No more midnight marathons spent trying to get someone set free from something that did not want to go from someone who never dealt with the original "why" as to the demon's access to their life.

My friend, who works with SRA and DID affected persons have found the Courts of Heaven to be "intercession on steroids!" She has found much more success and success with ease via the Courts of Heaven.

Many times, we are trying to remove something that still has a legal right to be present. It would be like someone trying to evict someone from a property that the resident has the legal rights to occupy. If you are dealing with an issue, let's find out the "why," Then, deal with it and get past this hurdle that may have hindered your spiritual walk. Let's continue.

Chapter 3
The Promise of Seeing

To know what God's Word says concerning a matter helps us establish the desire of God in our hearts and how we can attain that desire. If we are unsure of the will of God concerning spiritual seeing, we will have difficulty extending our faith toward being healed. I likely cannot attain what I cannot extend faith concerning.

God's Word on Spiritual Seeing

Therefore I also, after I heard of your faith in the Lord Jesus and your love for all the saints, ¹⁶ do not cease to give thanks for you, making mention of you in my prayers: ¹⁷ that the God of our Lord Jesus Christ, the Father of glory, may give to you the spirit of wisdom and revelation in the knowledge of Him, ¹⁸ **the eyes of your understanding being enlightened;** <u>that you may know</u> *what is the hope of His calling, what* are the riches of the glory of His inheritance in the saints, ¹⁹ and what is the exceeding greatness of His power toward us who believe, according to the working of His mighty power ²⁰ which He worked in Christ when He raised Him from the dead and seated Him at His right hand in the heavenly places, ²¹ far above all principality and power and might and dominion, and every name that is named, not only in this age but also in that which is to come. ²² And He put all things under His feet and gave Him to be head over all things to the church, ²³ which is His body, the fullness of Him who fills all in all. (Ephesians 1:15-23) (Emphasis mine)*

The purpose of your eyes being enlightened is so you will know!

Here is The Passion Translation of that passage:

¹⁵Because of this, since I first heard about your strong faith in the Lord Jesus Christ and your tender love toward all his devoted ones, ¹⁶ my heart is always full and overflowing with thanks to God for you as I constantly remember you in my prayers. ¹⁷ I pray that the Father of glory, the God of our Lord Jesus Christ, would impart to you the riches of the Spirit of wisdom and the Spirit of revelation to know him through your deepening intimacy with him. ¹⁸ I

*pray that **the light of God will illuminate the eyes of your imagination,** <u>flooding you with light, until you experience the full revelation</u> of the hope of his calling—that is, the wealth of God's glorious inheritances that he finds in us, his holy ones!* ^{19} *I pray that you will continually experience the immeasurable greatness of God's power made available to you through faith. Then your lives will be an advertisement of this immense power as it works through you! This is the mighty power* ^{20} *that was released when God raised Christ from the dead and exalted him to the place of highest honor and supreme authority in the heavenly realm!* ^{21} *And now he is exalted as first above every ruler, authority, government, and realm of power in existence! He is gloriously enthroned over every name that is ever praised, not only in this age but in the age that is coming!* ^{22} *And he alone is the leader and source of everything needed in the church. God has put everything beneath the authority of Jesus Christ and has given him the highest rank above all others.* ^{23} *And now we, his church, are his body on the earth and that which fills him who is being filled by it!* (Ephesians 1:18-23) (TPT) (Emphasis mine)

Your imagination is involved (see verse 18). It is how you paint the picture of what is revealed to your spirit.

If I were to ask you to describe your kitchen, most of you could do it. You know what cabinet the glasses are in. You know where the plates and bowls are. You know which drawer the utensils are in and in what position in the drawer. All these things, you can draw a picture of in your imagination and describe your kitchen to me. You can describe the wall color, the floor pattern, etc. Why because you have a memory and an imagination.

But how do I know that I just remember something? Of course, you remember something. You have not always been on earth. You existed with God before being birthed here, and you'll exist with God after you leave hear. You've already seen Heaven! That is why it is not so difficult to describe the beauty that is Heaven. You already have a frame of reference for it. God arranged that! [5]

> *Where there is **no vision, the people perish**: but he that keepeth the law, happy is he. (Proverbs 29:18) (KJV)*

A vision is something seen. A vision is typically seen with your spirit, not your natural eyes.

> *[16] But this is what was spoken by the prophet Joel: [17] 'And it shall come to pass in the last days, says God, that I will pour out of My Spirit on all flesh; your sons and your daughters shall prophesy, your young men **shall see visions**,*

---

[5] Proverbs 8:22-31

and your old men shall dream dreams. (Acts 2:16-17) (Emphasis mine)

*²⁵ For I know that my Redeemer lives, and He shall stand at last on the earth; ²⁶ And after my skin is destroyed, this I know, that **in my flesh I shall see God,** ²⁷ **whom I shall see for myself, and my eyes shall behold, and not another.** How my heart yearns within me! (Job 19:25-27) (Emphasis mine)*

Job understood that he was going to personally experience seeing God while on the earth.

*Oh, taste **and see** that the LORD is good; blessed is the man who trusts in Him! (Psalms 34:8) (Emphasis mine)*

*For with You is the fountain of life; in Your light **we see light**. (Psalms 36:9) (Emphasis mine)*

*¹ O God, You are my God; early will I seek You; My soul thirsts for You; my flesh longs for You In a dry and thirsty land where there is no water. ² So I have looked for You in the sanctuary, **to see Your power and Your glory**. (Psalms 63:1-2) (Emphasis mine)*

*The heavens declare His righteousness, and all the peoples **see His glory**. (Psalms 97:6) (Emphasis mine)*

> *Blessed are the pure in heart, **for they shall see God**. (Matthew 5:8) (Emphasis mine)*

We have this promise from Jesus, and since He is the one who purifies our hearts, we qualify to see God. Religion may tell you that you cannot see God, but Jesus said we could. I choose what Jesus said. How about you?

> *[16] **But blessed are your eyes for they see**, and your ears for they hear; [17] for assuredly, I say to you that many prophets and righteous men desired to see what you see, and did not see it, and to hear what you hear, and did not hear it. (Matthew 13:16-17) (Emphasis mine)*

Jesus spoke this promise to his disciples. Notice that it included seeing AND hearing. Let's lay claim to that promise!

> *And He said, "To you, it **has been given to know the mysteries of the kingdom of God**, but to the rest it is given in parables, that 'Seeing they may not see, and hearing they may not understand.' (Luke 8:10) (Emphasis mine)*

To know mysteries will require spiritual insight. Spiritual sight is a major component of knowing mysteries—it is essential equipment.

> *Jesus answered and said to him, "Most assuredly, I say to you, unless one is born again, he cannot **see the kingdom of God**." John 3:3 (Emphasis mine)*

We need to "see" the kingdom of God! Not just read about it. Our experience with the realms of Heaven must be personalized.

> *For now, **we see in a mirror**, dimly, but then face to face. Now I know in part, but then I shall know just as I also am known. (1 Corinthians 13:12)*

The greater our love level, the greater our seeing ability should be!

That does not preclude the fact that just because someone can see in the realm of the spirit that they must be full of love. I have met exceptions to this rule. Many who see well have a preoccupation with judgment and the idea that God is angry with us.

Judgment is never God's first response – love is!

> *[9] and to **make all see what is the fellowship of the mystery**, which from the beginning of the ages has been hidden in God who created all things through Jesus Christ; [10] to the intent that now **the manifold wisdom of God might be made known by the church** to the principalities and powers in the heavenly places, [11] according to the eternal purpose which He accomplished in Christ Jesus our Lord, [12] in whom we have boldness and access*

with confidence through faith in Him. (Ephesians 3:9-12) (Emphasis mine)

To accomplish this, we must be able to see. God wants us to know His will. Being able to see spiritually would facilitate that.

Chapter 4
Obstacles to Seeing – Part 1

Accusations & False Verdicts

My work with clients around the globe in advocacy sessions in the Courts of Heaven finds similar issues everywhere. Although some countries have unique situations, the basic things people face is universal. One of those arenas involves being able to see in the realm of the spirit. Some cannot see at all, while others see only dimly. As we searched for solutions on this issue, we have uncovered some things that will be helpful, and that will help you experience what it is to see clearly in the realm of the spirit.

Although the spiritual hearing is vital too, we will be focusing this book on spiritual sight. The principles unveiled will apply to spiritual seeing as well. Dr. Mark Virkler, founder of New York-based Communion with God (www.cwgministries.org) has excellent resources in developing spiritual hearing with what he calls, The *Four Keys to Hearing God's Voice*.

Often, we find ourselves spiritually blind but have no understanding of why. As I began to search this out, I found some common culprits. First, I will list the most common ones, then unpack them one-by-one so you can come to a place of freedom regarding your spiritual sight. May your testimony be like the man blind from birth, whom Jesus healed:

> *One thing I know: that though I was blind, now I see." (John 9:25)*

This man did not care about the politicizing going on around him – he was glad he could see!

Now, let's begin to deal with some of the obstacles to our spiritual seeing.

1) Accusations

The need to deal with accusations against us doesn't end with the Mercy Court. Accusations against our sight must dismantled in every arena. The purpose of an accusation is to divert you from your purpose. If you are cannot see spiritually, and the accusation is that you will never be able to see; if that accusation is embraced and not dismantled, you will not be able to fulfill your purpose.

Sample Accusations

- You have no right to see!
- You are too young to be seeing angels.
- You aren't spiritual enough to see.
- If you do that, you'll start seeing demons and junk!

Follow the four-step process I espouse to get accusations dismantled in your life so you can move ahead.

The Four Steps

1. Agree with the adversary (Matthew 5:25-26)
2. Confess it as sin (1 John 1:9)
3. Repent (Proverbs 28:13)
4. Apply the Blood of Jesus (1 John 1:7)

These simple steps have helped many enter freedom from the power the accusations were placed against their lives, no matter what the accusation was.

In some cases, entire families are under the pressure of accusations that are keeping the whole family from experiencing God's best for their lives regarding their health. In this situation, the father, mother (or both) can step into their role as priests and deal with the accusations. Deal with *every* accusation.

Recovering Sight[6]

1. Request access to the Court of Cancellations once you have dealt with the accusations[7]
2. Repent for embracing any lie that has affected your ability to see in the spirit
3. Ask for forgiveness
4. Forgive those making the accusations
5. Bless them
6. Release them
7. Request restoration of your sight
8. Request any covering over your sight be removed
9. Begin to see!

False Verdicts

Another thing we discovered that often blocked spiritual seeing in a person was the issue of false verdicts against their ability to see. Sometimes a person (or their entire family line) had a false verdict related (for instance) to the inability of their body to see spiritually. Despite doing everything, they knew to do; they were still no better. As we probed this issue, we found that false verdicts needed to get overturned to bring a resolution to the persons' situation.

---

[6] See the Obstacles to Seeing - Accusations process chart in the Appendix.

[7] Accusations are generally dealt with in the Mercy Court, but may be dealt with outside of any court and simply present testimony of the fact you have dealt with the accusations in whatever court you are involved in.

Sample False Verdicts

- Seeing in the spirit is only for prophets and seers.
- Small children are not permitted to see in the spirit
- Seeing in the spirit is only for saints.

Clearing False Verdicts[8]

The solution is simple:

- Access the Court of Appeals
- Request the overturning of the false verdict(s)
- Repent on behalf of those creating the false verdict originally
- Forgive them
- Bless them
- Release them
- Request that the false verdict be replaced with a righteous verdict on your behalf.
- Ask that your spiritual sight be restored
- Request any covering over your sight be removed
- Begin to see!

---

[8] See the Obstacles to Seeing - False Verdicts process chart in the Appendix.

Familial False Verdicts

On occasion, you will find family units where a false verdict is in place. False verdicts are not always the case as generational iniquities may also be involved.

When that has occurred, we want to uncover the source event where the false verdict became enacted. Typically, a sin was committed that had, as part of its consequence – spiritual blindness.

Sample Familial False Verdicts

- It is not permitted for the Jones family to see spiritual things.
- The iniquity of the Jones family disqualifies them from seeing spiritual things.

To clear these familial false verdicts, we will repent for the sin and forgive the one(s) who introduced this condition into the family line, bless and release them, and ask for our spiritual sight to be restored and the tarp removed hindering our ability to see.

Clearing Familial False Verdicts

- Access the Court of Appeals
- Request the overturning of the false verdict(s)
- Repent on behalf of those creating the false verdict originally
- Forgive them
- Bless them
- Release them

- Request that the false verdict be replaced with a righteous verdict on your behalf.
- Ask that your spiritual sight be restored
- Request any covering over your sight be removed
- Begin to see!

Chapter 5
Obstacles to Seeing – Part 2

Covenants or Oaths

Sometimes covenants or oaths are in place that is binding us to spiritual blindness. Typically, these may be of the Freemasonry variety or any number of other flavors. They all have one aim – to destroy your life and purpose.

As I mentioned in an earlier chapter, the Freemasonry hoodwink is often the most impactful covenant on spiritual seeing in my experience.

Regardless of the demonic source of the covenants, it can be resolved in the Courts of Heaven. As we do in many other procedures in the courts, we first must step into a place of repentance.

Repentance is not optional in the Courts of Heaven!

> *The more repentant we are,
> the more progress we can make
> in the Courts of Heaven.*

What we must realize about covenants and oaths is that they stand until dissolved. They have legal standing in the realm of the spirit that must recognized, so it has to be resolved and dissolved.

> *Covenants and oaths
> stand until dissolved.*

Understanding that those who entered into these covenants originally were often unaware of the full ramifications of these deadly agreements; this will help us to be able to forgive and release them from what they did more easily. When you realize that many things were results of their brokenness and pain, it makes it much easier to walk in compassion toward them and extend compassion to them.

We access the Court of Cancellations. Although we may not know the originator of the covenant, we can forgive them anyway. We ask Holy Spirit to unveil to us who was responsible or how many generations back in our lineage this occurred. We then repent for the initial sin of making the covenant or oath. We repent for those who enforced or perpetuated it and forgive the person for the sin. We bless them and release them. Request the Lord release you and your bloodline from the consequences of the covenant or oath. We also may ask the Lord to bring restoration to the heirs of those who may have been victims of this person enacting this covenant.

Abolishing Covenants or Oaths[9]

1. Request access to the Court of Cancellations
2. Ask Holy Spirit to unveil the originator of the covenant or oath. (If related to Freemasonry, repent for you or your ancestor(s) who put on the hoodwink and took oaths against their spiritual sight and yours.)
3. Repent for making the covenant or oath initially
4. Repent for enforcing or perpetuating the covenant or oath
5. Forgive them
6. Bless them
7. Release them
8. Request the Lord release you and your bloodline from the consequences of the covenant or oath.
9. Ask the Lord to bring restoration to the heirs of those who may have been victims of this person enacting this covenant.
10. Request the restoration of your spiritual sight
11. Begin to see.

---

[9] See the Obstacles to Seeing - Covenants-Oaths process chart in the Appendix.

Covenant of Death

In Isaiah 28,[10] we read of the covenant of death that has come about by the wickedness of an ancestor(s). The Lord wants any covenant of death (or any covenant with death) dissolved in our lives, so we do not live subject to the demands of death. Death will exact a toll on anyone under its subjection. Unless canceled it will continue to bear its terrible fruit in our lives and families. We access the Court of Cancellations and request this wicked covenant be annulled, and any agreement with Sheol also be canceled. Often these covenants with death have been enacted by our ancestors as part of wicked trades they performed or profane worship in which they engaged.

In some cultures, the demon gods demanded the covenant of death be enacted to allow them to periodically exact payment (usually in the form of human life) so that the innocent bloodshed would help feed the demons lust. In many places, you will notice a pattern of young people dying tragically just before (or immediately after) their high school or college graduation. These events tied to a covenant of death must be annulled.

---

[10] Isaiah 28:18

Abolishing the Covenant of Death[11]

1. Request access to the Court of Cancellations
2. Ask Holy Spirit to unveil the originator of the covenant of death
3. Repent for those making this Covenant of Death initially
4. Repent for those enforcing or perpetuating the covenant
5. Forgive them
6. Bless them
7. Release them
8. Repent for your sin in the matter
9. Request the Lord cleanse and release you and your bloodline from the consequences of the covenant of death
10. Ask the Lord to bring restitution to yourself and anyone else affected by the negative consequences of this covenant of death
11. Request the restoration of your spiritual sight
12. Request a Covenant of Life be enacted on behalf of you and your generations
13. Begin to see!

Covenants or Oaths Through Organizations

It is possible that our sight was impacted by ties to organizations, denominations, fraternities, sororities, or even civil or religious covenants (including Freemasonry

---

[11] See the Obstacles to Seeing - Covenant of Death Release process chart in the Appendix.

and similar organizations). We may have made a promise to someone in authority regarding our seeing ability. If it was an ungodly or unhealthy agreement, we need to repent and ask that any covenant that is not in line with the laws and will of God be annulled in our behalf. Adapt the procedures above to find freedom. It may help to be quite specific concerning the organization and the covenant or oath.

For instance, in Freemasonry, the candidate allows a hoodwink (blindfold) to be placed over his eyes. He is making an oath to only see Freemasonry's version of light (which is no light at all)!

Chapter 6
Obstacles to Seeing – Part 3

Ownership Claims

On rare occasions, we find someone with an ownership claim in the form of a title which often occurs because they were dedicated to Satan. The false title is simply interfering with their ability to see or to see clearly. It is quite probable that they have ownership claims upon their life that has given right to spiritual blindness to afflict them. Only with their permission are you able to get these ownership claims resolved; however, they CAN be resolved. Repentance and renunciation as well as divorcing from the entity are involved. We also need to render forgiveness to get the false title abolished and the right title instated with the Lord Jehovah as the person's full and rightful owner.

Claims like this are not false in the sense they are not legal, because the individual has given the entity permission to "own" them. They have surrendered themselves to that situation. The process for full ownership typically works through stages.

The first stage is simply the introduction of the idea into the person's life. The degree of the embrace of the idea can determine whether it places a lien upon them spiritually or whether they reject the idea and recover from its effects. Whenever an ungodly thought or idea comes into my mind, I can embrace it, or I can resist it. I can refuse to allow it the right to dominate my life or not.

Many times, people assume that we must succumb to every thought or idea that comes along. That is not the case. We do not have to succumb to these things. Introduction of a thought or idea is often the testing ground of the enemy to see if he can do more damage. Our first responses to the thoughts or ideas must be in the realm of the spirit first. We can reject them outright and request the blood cover the thought or idea.

Liens or False Titles Against Our Sight

When someone has an ownership claim (whether a lien, false title, note or lease agreement) that is impacting their life, we must forgive those who placed the ownership claim on our life. We deal with these things in the Court of Titles and Deeds.

Releasing Liens[12]

First, I request access to the Court of Titles and Deeds. Then, I follow this simple procedure:

1. I forgive them (John 20:23)[13]
2. I bless them (Matthew 5:44-45)[14]
3. I release them (Luke 6:37)[15]

When talking about John 20:23, I ask how many have ever heard a sermon on that verse. I think I have seen two hands raised of persons who had heard a sermon on forgiving other people from that passage. The power of that instruction is huge. As Protestants, we have dismissed what the Catholics and Anglicans have understood in some measure. We can forgive the sins of someone. It is a priestly function, and we are kings and priests. If I want forgiveness, I need to forgive. If I want to be blessed, then I must be willing to bless. If I want to be released, I then will gladly release.

---

[12] See the Obstacles to Seeing - Ownership Claims - Liens process chart in the Appendix.

[13] If you forgive the sins of any, they are forgiven them; if you retain the sins of any, they are retained." (NKJV)

[14] 44 However, I say to you, love your enemy, bless the one who curses you, do something wonderful for the one who hates you, bf and respond to the very ones who persecute you by praying for them. 45 For that will reveal your identity as children of your heavenly Father. (TPT)

[15] "Judge not, and you shall not be judged. Condemn not, and you shall not be condemned. Forgive (release), and you will be forgiven (released). (NKJV)

In forgiving you are removing the hook, the sin had to hold you or the other person in bondage. In blessing, I'm unfolding the goodness of God toward the person. It has nothing to do with whether they deserve this or not. We, in and of ourselves, don't deserve the goodness of God either; and in releasing them, I take them off the hook, and they are free to no longer sin after that manner again.

Removing the hook of sin is what Jesus did toward the woman caught in the act of adultery[16]. He released her from the hook adultery had in her life, and she was then free to no longer be an adulteress. Her partner did not partake of that forgiveness and likely continued in the sin with someone else.

We can also experience liens from emotions or conditions we find ourselves in, and in some cases, we have liens as a result of an entity (usually demonic) for which we need freedom. The process charts for liens, detail the path to freedom.

Once we have done those three steps, we also request the following:

4. That the lien to be marked satisfied by the blood of Jesus.
5. That the Lord restore our spiritual sight.
6. If necessary, we repent for embracing fear on any level.

---

[16] John 8:2-11

7. Request any covering over your spiritual eyes to be removed.

Abolishing False Titles[17]

If a false title, we follow the same procedure. Someone is claiming ownership of your sight. It could be a person, demon, entity, or even an organization (i.e., Freemasonry, churches, clubs, military organizations).

As before, we forgive those responsible for the false title, bless them, and release them; Then request the old title be abolished and a new title issued with the Lord Jehovah made the Lord over our seeing. Ask the Lord to restore our spiritual sight and remove any tarp over our ability to see.

1. Request access to the Court of Titles and Deeds
2. Request a transfer of title from whomever to the Lord Jehovah
3. I forgive them (John 20:23)
4. I bless them (Matthew 5:44-45)
5. I release them (Luke 6:37)
6. Request the false title be abolished
7. Request a new title be issued
8. Request our sight be restored
9. Request the removal of any tarp
10. Begin to see!

---

[17] See the Obstacles to Seeing - Ownership Claims – False Titles process chart in the Appendix.

Other process charts designate the path to freedom from false notes, and lease agreements. These are not as common as the lien, but on occasion will be identified so you can deal with them.[18]

---

[18] See the Obstacles to Seeing process charts in the Appendix.

Chapter 7
Obstacles to Seeing– Part 4

Curses & Generational Iniquities

Sometimes curses are in play concerning our sight. At times we have been the recipient of a curse from any number of sources – witchcraft, sorcery, charismatic witchcraft, ancestral worship situations, and more. We must break the curses affecting our ability to see and hear. It may be that someone spoke over your life and cursed you. We need to get that curse broken off your life.

Request access to the Court of Cancellations and ask Holy Spirit to reveal every curse. Then, request the cancellation of every curse affecting our sight. If you are having trouble identifying the possible curses, ask a trusted person to assist you in identifying any curses. If the person is a seer, that can help immensely although that is not essential to you getting things dealt with. Do not avoid doing it just because you do not have a seer. If necessary, contact our offices and set up a Personal Advocacy Session (www.courtsofheaven.net). Once the curses are identified, it is time to move to the next steps.

If we need to repent of embracing the impact of the curse, then do so. If we need to forgive the person(s) who invoked the curse, then do so.

Freedom from Curses on Our Sight

I request access to the Court of Cancellations. I am requesting the cancellation of the curse of _____ from off my life that I am being impacted by.

I repent for the originating sin, I forgive, bless & release the one(s) who introduced it into the family line. I repent for my sin in the matter.

I ask you, Just Judge to cleanse it from me and my family line and release me and my family line from the consequences of this curse.

I also request restitution to me and anyone else affected by the negative consequences of this curse.

Additionally, I request the complete restoration of my spiritual sight.

Finally, you are asking the Just Judge to restore your spiritual sight. You may need to perform a prophetic act of taking cleaning your spiritual glasses or cleaning the inside of your spiritual windshield (just like you would do on your car) to remove any fogginess to our seeing.

Removing Curses on Our Sight[19]

1. Request access to the Court of Cancellations
2. Request Holy Spirit's help to identify any curses. (Ask a trusted friend to help you, if necessary)
3. Request cancellation of every curse affecting our spiritual sight
4. Repent for whomever initiated this curse in your family line
5. Forgive the person(s) who invoked the curse
6. Bless them
7. Release them
8. Repent (if necessary) of embracing the impact of the curse
9. Ask the Just Judge to cleanse it from you and your family line and release you and your family from the consequences of the curse
10. Request restitution to you and anyone else affected by the negative consequences of this curse, and finally
11. Request the complete restoration of my spiritual sight
12. Begin to see!

---

[19] See the Obstacles to Seeing - Curses process chart in the Appendix.

Generational Iniquities

Iniquities are patterns of sin that have gone on so long that we no longer see them as sin. We are no longer convicted by what we are doing.

Every sin has a consequence. For example, anger will often affect the liver. Anxiousness will affect the heart and other parts of our body. Grief will impact our lungs. In almost every situation of sickness or disease, a spiritual root cause is to blame. The Courts of Healing and Heaven's Hospital help us to deal with the legal rights holding things in place so we can step into a place of freedom and wholeness.

What if somewhere in your ancestry, someone made it their job to blind others physically or spiritually? Is it possible that a harvesting effect has come into play? I think it is possible. In which case, we need to repent for the sin, forgive the perpetrator, and request restoration of all victim and their family line lost.

With any iniquity, we must repent, forgive those who introduced it into our family lines, forgive those who perpetrated it throughout the generations and ask for the forgiveness of God and for him to purify our DNA, our family tree, and our bodies and introduce us to wholeness.

Removing Generational Iniquities Affecting our Sight[20]

1. Request access to the Court of Cancellations
2. Ask Holy Spirit to unveil the originator of the iniquity in the bloodline
3. Repent for the original sin which introduced this iniquity to the bloodline
4. Repent for any who enforced or perpetrated the iniquity in the bloodline
5. Forgive them
6. Bless them
7. Release them
8. Request the Lord release you and your bloodline from the consequences of the generational iniquity.
9. Ask the Lord to bring restoration to the heirs of those who may have been victims of this person enacting this iniquity.
10. Ask the Lord to restore your sight
11. Begin to see!

---

[20] See the Obstacles to Seeing – Generational Iniquities process chart in the Appendix.

Chapter 8
Obstacles to Seeing – Part 5

In this chapter we will finalize talking about the various possible obstacles to spiritual seeing. Many of you by this point in the book have already experienced improvement. If you have not, do not give up! Hang on a little longer. Also, don't allow frustration to set it. You were designed to be able to see and you shall. Let's look at a few more possible obstacles.

Trophy Room

At times, the enemy has made of spectacle of people and in a sense has placed them in a trophy case in the Trophy Room of Hell. Those captivated in this place need to be freed. The process we have used successfully is as follows:

1. Request access to the Court of Appeals
2. Repent for anything that would have placed the person in this place of imprisonment.
3. From the Court of Appeals request a Certificate of Freedom

4. Request angelic assistance to take you to the trophy room
5. Receive the Certificate and the key to the trophy case
6. Request angelic assistance to take you to the Trophy Room
7. Unlock the person from the trophy case and bring them out of the trophy case
8. Ask the angel to smash the trophy case
9. Take them out of the trophy room and establish them in the realms of Heaven
10. Request release of your spiritual sight
11. Begin to see!

Once they are out of the trophy case and the trophy room you may need to deal with broken heartedness. Simply follow the instructions of Holy Spirit.

Regions of Captivity

You may have felt as if you have been held captive regarding your spiritual sight. It was not an ownership claim *per se* but it has hindered you nonetheless. Freedom, in this situation involves a series of prophetic acts as well as dealing with the captivity.

Captivity by the enemy is permitted as long as *our* sin (or our ancestors' sin) gave the legal rights for it. However, once we repent for our sins and/or the sins of our ancestors, the rights of the enemy to hold us captive are removed. We then apply for a Writ of Habeus Corpus which is accomplished in the Court of Appeals.

__Bring my soul out of prison__, that I may praise Your name; the righteous shall surround me, for You shall deal bountifully with me. (Psalms 142:7) (Emphasis mine)

Certificate of Freedom

The Certificate of Freedom is what is issued when someone is freed from unlawful imprisonment. In the American court system it is known as a Writ of Habeus Corpus. This writ[21] contests the imprisonment of a person or class of persons and brings the person before the court in order to have a hearing on the imprisonment. If the claims of unlawful imprisonment are found to be valid, then the prisoner is ordered to be released. However, if the claims are found to be valid that the prisoner is being held in captivity, then the prisoner will remain in captivity. Once the paperwork has been issued (either a Certificate of Freedom or Writ of Habeus Corpus), request the key to the cell.

In this case, request angelic assistance, step into the place of captivity with the angel or Jesus, unlock the cell, and release them from the shackles and chains binding them. Remove the shackles from around their neck, around their waist, from off their wrists and ankles. Also, remove the blindfold from their eyes or the helmet upon their head so they can begin to see clearly. Then, bring them out of that place of captivity. [You can do this for

---

[21] Writ – a written directive issued by a court

yourself (if necessary) as you will not be alone because Jesus or an angel will assist you.] Once they are out of the place of captivity, ask that they be established in the realms of Heaven and request the complete restoration of their spiritual sight.[22]

The same concept can be used for those who are entrapped in a deep pit, the miry clay, the doors of the shadow of death, desert places, the gates of pain, place of jackals, land of forgetfulness, the region of death, pit of destruction, pit of iniquity, and the pits of desperation.[23]

Jeanettte Strauss, author of *From The Courtroom of Heaven To the Throne Of Grace and Mercy*,[24] found the following scripture to be quite valuable in seeing her daughter released from the deep bondage she had gotten into:

> *Shall the prey be taken from the mighty, or the captives of the righteous be delivered? But thus says the LORD: "Even the captives of the mighty shall be taken away,* [25] *and the prey of the terrible be delivered; for I will contend with him who contends with you, and I will save your children. (Isaiah 49:24-25)*

---

[22] See the Obstacles to Seeing - Regions of Captivity process chart in the Appendix.

[23] Ana Mendez Farrell's book *Regions of Captivity* is an excellent resource on this concept.

[24] Available on Amazon and other retailers.

If we, by our choices, step into the enemies' camp, it should come as no surprise that we end up in captivity. This passage promises deliverance for the captives, but that will only come by following the rules!

> *For I know the thoughts that I think toward you, says the LORD, thoughts of peace and not of evil, to give you a future and a hope. Then you will call upon Me and go and pray to Me, and I will listen to you. And you will seek Me and find Me, when you search for Me with all your heart. I will be found by you, says the LORD, and I will bring you back from your captivity; I will gather you from all the nations and from all the places where I have driven you, says the LORD, and I will bring you to the place from which I cause you to be carried away captive. (Jeremiah 29:11-14)*

We must repent of that which brought us into captivity in the first place. That involves confession of the sin (saying about the sin, what God says about it), and repentance – a turning from the sin and the lifestyle of it.

The children of Israel found themselves in captivity as the result of bad choices. That is the essence of what brings most of us into captivity. The good news is, we can be freed!

Vows Against Our Seeing

At some point in our lives, we may have made a vow to never see spiritually. Often this occurs when we have been afraid as a result of something we saw. We also make vows to shut down our imagination not realizing that it is the interface God uses to bring things from the spirit to our soul. It is not unlike the monitor on your computer, which translates the bits and bytes into something you can comprehend in this realm.

We must repent for any ungodly vows we have made. If we made any ungodly trading floor agreements; we need to repent and request the cancellation of any trade and the cessation of any consequences related to them.

Again, if we need to forgive someone or some organization, do so. Then request the restoration of your spiritual sight and the removal of any tarp hindering our seeing.

Release from Vows Against our Sight

1. Request access to the Court of Cancellations
2. Repent for making any vow that was not in line with the purposes or will of God
3. Repent for enforcing or perpetuating the vow
4. Repent for embracing any lie leading you to make the vow originally
5. Ask forgiveness

6. Request the Lord release you (and your bloodline)[25] from the consequences of the vow
7. Ask the Lord to bring restoration to your spiritual sight
8. Begin to see!

Shutting Down Our Imagination

Part of making vows concerning our spiritual sight often involves misunderstandings about our imagination.

Much of the body of Christ has bought into the lie that "imagination is bad!" That is a lie! Imagination is what God uses to communicate via our spirit. To see a vision is to have your spirit communicate to your soul via the imagination. Like the monitor on your computer or the screen on your phone, your imagination part of your soul takes the information from Heaven and places it in picture form. You use your imagination to form pictures which is a function of the right brain hemisphere, which is more artistic and musical and NOT logic based. Logical thinking occurs from the left-brain hemisphere. Seeing with the eyes of our spirit involves the right brain. Our logical thinking must take a back seat to this process.

It is OK to imagine. It is OK to form pictures in your mind. Remember, we now have the mind of Christ. Unless you are continuously filling your mind with garbage, garbage will not be coming out. If it does, apply

---

[25] If they were part of the vow.

the blood to those images within your imagination so the images are removed from your mind.

Clearing Religious Mindsets

If religion has told you it was dangerous to see in the spirit, stop right now and repent of embracing that lie and renounce it. Ask God to forgive you and to restore your sight! Then, begin to see.

1. Access Court of Cancellations
2. Repent of embracing the lies of religion
3. Request and receive forgiveness
4. Request the cancellation of every mindset and covenant hindering you
5. Ask God to restore your sight
6. Begin to see!

Jesus depended upon seeing for revelation and instruction, according to John 8:38:

> *Yet the truths I speak **I've seen and received in my Father's presence**. (TPT) (Emphasis mine)*

If spiritual sight was important to Jesus, it should be just as important to us.

Kay Tolman, in her book, *Moved with Compassion*, stated this:

> *"The only way to see the Father is through right-brain imagery.*

> *Some ministers express concern about performing a new age practice when working with right-brain imagery. New age practices counterfeit the real things of the Kingdom of God. If they didn't have value, they wouldn't be copied. Just because the enemy has copied something God intended to bring greater intimacy with Him, doesn't mean we throw the practice out. Instead, we use it properly. One way to ensure the enemy doesn't infect a holy process, and to ease your mind, just consecrate the eyes of your heart to God." (Tolman, 2017)[26] p.115*

Let's stop throwing the baby out with the bathwater and begin to maximize the capabilities God has built into us. We must learn to engage with our right hemisphere to bring healing to traumas.

> *"Research has shown that mental practice – imagination, visualization, deep through, and reflection – produces the same physical changes in the brain as it would [by] physically carrying out the same imagined processes," says Dr. Carolyn Leaf in "Who Switched Off My Brain?" "When Jesus heals a wound for a trauma survivor using right brain imagery, physically,*

---

[26] P. 115

it has the same effect on the brain as though it really happened! (Tolman, 2017)[27]

Once we understand how powerful right-brain imagery and visualization is, we also can understand why Satan would try to keep this valuable tool away from the body of Christ.

When Jesus heals a wound for a trauma survivor using right brain imager, physically, it has the same effect on the brain as though it actually happened!

In the chapter "The Observer Effect" (coming up) we look at this concept from the quantum physics understandings we now possess.

The Results

The several categories we have been talking about in this chapter will help you work through the problems of spiritual blindness and how it gained entrance into our lives. We have seen person after person who discovered they were indeed seeing after following the guidelines we shared with them.

Let's review the list:

---

[27] P. 116

- Accusations
- False verdicts
- Covenants or oaths
- Ownership claims
- Curses
- Generational iniquities
- Regions of Captivity
- Vows against our seeing

Other Causes

In rare instances, individuals have additional causes that have hindered their ability to see spiritually. I am sure others exist, but these are ones with which we have had some experience.

Anger Toward God

At times, we must deal with any anger toward God. We must repent of holding anger toward God and repent on behalf of those in the family tree that has had anger toward God -- probably about everyone could be included on some level!

This anger is like a permission slip for sickness or disease as well as spiritual blindness. Many forms of cancer seem to have this type of anger at its root.

Unforgiveness

We cannot underestimate the impact of unforgiveness on our spiritual health. Henry Wright, in his book, *A More Excellent Way* teaches extensively on how unforgiveness impacts the body and allows destruction to occur in our lives. Like anger, Unforgiveness is another permission slip for sickness, disease, and spiritual blindness to reside in our bodies. We need not let it go any further. We need to repent and ask for God to bring restoration to us and every cell within us.

As time goes on, other reasons hindering our spiritual sight will be uncovered, but the ones covered thus far are significant. We will add others as information and wisdom is unveiled to us.

Chapter 9
The Observer Effect

In the field of quantum physics, one of the most basic tenets (if not THE most basic tenet) is known as "the observer effect." Simply stated, the observer effect can be defined this way:

What I observe changes what I am observing.

The very act of looking at something causes it to change. Invisible waves of energy or potential change simply by looking at them. As scientists try to measure these waves of energy, they change from waves of energy into a particle (or particles) – something concrete. It is no longer a series of waves – it has become substance. It is something we can observe in our dimension of time and space. It is matter.

Wave Function Collapse

Scientists call this transformation where the energy waves collapse into a particle, "wave function collapse."

It is taking something invisible and making it visible. Something unseen is now seen. We first see it via our imagination using visualization, however.

Within the quantum realm, any possible outcome is available at any and every moment in time.

That is how physicists define it. We need to pause and meditate on that statement. We would call that faith. In Hebrews 11:1:

*Now faith is the substance of things hoped for, **the evidence of things not seen [but seen with the eyes of our spirit]**. (Hebrews 11:1) (Emphasis mine)*

*Jesus said to him, "If you can believe, **all things are possible to him who believes.**" (Mark 9:23) (Emphasis mine)*

Our believing is facilitated by our seeing the matter done via visualization. Visualization is NOT a curse word. It is a valuable technique for accessing the Kingdom realm of Heaven.

*(As it is written, "I have made you a father of many nations") in the presence of Him whom he believed–God, who gives life to the dead **and calls those things which do not exist as though they did**. (Romans 4:17) (Emphasis mine.)*

You can call those things because you see them with what Paul called the "eyes of your understanding."

> *17 That the God of our Lord Jesus Christ, the Father of glory, may give to you the spirit of wisdom and revelation in the knowledge of Him, 18 the eyes of your understanding being enlightened; that you may know what is the hope of His calling, what are the riches of the glory of His inheritance in the saints. (Ephesians 1:17-18) (Emphasis mine)*

We have revelation because the eyes of our understanding are made to see (which is what "enlightened" means).

Everything we need, now or in the future, is already available to us. We have this promise:

> *Blessed be the God and Father of our Lord Jesus Christ,* **who has blessed us with every spiritual blessing in the heavenly places [the unseen realm] in Christ.** *(Ephesians 1:3) (Emphasis mine) (Additions mine)*

They are unseen to our natural eyes, but not to our spiritual eyes.

> *Grace to you and peace be multiplied in the knowledge of God and of Jesus our Lord; 3 seeing that his divine power* **has granted unto us all things that pertain unto life and godliness**, *through the knowledge of him that*

called us by his own glory and virtue. (2 Peter 1:2-3) (Emphasis mine)

The ability to see with our spiritual eyes is vital equipment for our walk with God. By spiritually seeing we can tap into the revelation God has for us.

We, in the body of Christ, have been so "Word-oriented" (which is a left-brained function) that we have ignored the understanding of that Word that comes from exercising right-brained function.

Everything we need is available. God has provided *everything*. Our challenge has been in learning how to get what is in Heaven to manifest in the earth. Quantum physics is explaining how things work that the Scriptures have been telling us. These glory waves of potential need to collapsing into our reality—into our realm of time and space. What is in Heaven needs to manifest in the earth.

*It is by faith we understand that the world was fashioned by the word of God, and **thus the visible was made out of the invisible.** (Hebrews 11:3) (Moffatt[28]) (Emphasis mine)*

---

[28] The Bible: James Moffatt Translation by James A R Moffatt, Kregel Publications, Grand Rapids, Michigan, USA, 1994

> *What is unseen*
> *needs to become seen.*

Scientists refer to this phenomenon of the invisible becoming visible as "wave function collapse;" this is what happens when we pray. The unseen becomes seen.

> *We see it with our spirit, then we can*
> *see it in the natural arena.*

Give us this day our daily bread. (Matthew 6:11)

The provision that is in Heaven manifests in the earth through food, water, finances, etc. That is *why* we pray.

If I am sick, I look at what the Word says about my situation "by His stripes I was healed,"[29] and as I grasp what He has said concerning me – as I see it with the eyes of my heart, my situation changes. I go from sickness to health. I "see" it (I observe it) and the situation changes—wave function collapse.

As we see with our spiritual eyes, we see what Heaven sees about me. Heaven's version of me is of a person healed, whole, glorious, without weakness or illness dominating my body. As I see that, I am changed.

But we all, with unveiled face, beholding as in a mirror the glory of the Lord, **are being**

---

[29] 1 Peter 2:24

> ***transformed into the same image*** *from glory to glory, just as by the Spirit of the Lord. (2 Corinthians 3:18) (Emphasis mine)*

My observation (seeing with my spirit) will result in transformation!

What is potential in Heaven, is collapsed into this realm, and I become what is Heaven's version of Me.

> *If then you were raised with Christ, **seek [observe] those things which are above**, where Christ is, sitting at the right hand of God. ² Set your mind [your sight] on things above, not on things on the earth. ³ For you died, and your life is hidden with Christ in God. ⁴ When Christ who is our life appears, then **you also will appear with Him in glory [in a transformed state of being]**. (Colossians 3:1-4) (Emphasis mine) (Additions mine)*

That is why we put off the things that hinder our transformation. Let us read a little further:

> *Therefore, put to death your members which are on the earth: fornication, uncleanness, passion, evil desire, and covetousness, which is idolatry. ⁶ Because of these things the wrath of God is coming upon the sons of disobedience, ⁷ in which you yourselves once walked when you lived in them. ⁸ But now you yourselves are to*

*put off all these: anger, wrath, malice, blasphemy, filthy language out of your mouth. ⁹ Do not lie to one another, since you have put off the old man with his deeds, ¹⁰ and have **put on the new man who is renewed in knowledge according to the image of Him who created him.** (Colossians 3:5-10) (Emphasis mine)*

Observation brings transformation!

What we observe—manifests.

The works of the flesh Paul just mentioned create the wrong images in our mind – images that bring destruction to ourselves, our relationships, and our lives.

We must behold
that which is life-giving,
not death producing!

Jesus said that he did what he saw his Father do and said what he heard his Father say. He observed what his father was doing, agreed with it, and it manifested in the earth.

*"Again, I say to you that if two of you agree on earth concerning **anything that they ask, it will be done for them** by My Father in heaven. (Matthew 18:19) (Emphasis mine)*

The word "ask" implies a search for something hidden–something desired. Because we come into agreement with Heaven, the hidden becomes manifest in the earth.

> *When you are praying over a matter, see with your spiritual eyes what it is you desire. Once you see it, come into an agreement with Heaven so that it can manifest.*

We have made it much more difficult than it is. We need agree with Heaven; Heaven is waiting on us! When we see via the realm of the spirit, we are visualizing the unseen.

> *The purpose of such visualization is to cause the unseen to become seen.*

Once seen in the spirit, begin to release it in the earth by the words of your mouth. Let your mouth agree with what your spirit sees so that it can come forth in the earth; to speak what you do not see is presumptuous.

In the Gospel of Mark, Jesus explains how it works:

So, Jesus answered and said to them, "Have faith in God [trust the process God has instituted]. 23 For assuredly, I say to you, whoever says to this mountain, 'Be removed and be cast into the sea,' and does not doubt in *his heart, but **believes [he is able to see with his spiritual eyes the thing desired] that those things he says will be done, he will have whatever he says [when his words are an expression of his agreement with Heaven].** ²⁴ Therefore I say to you, whatever things you ask **when you pray, believe that you receive them,** and **you will have them**. (Mark 11:22-24) (Emphasis mine) (Additions mine)*

In the last chapter of Luke, Jesus instructs his followers to wait in Jerusalem until they are endued with the power of the Holy Spirit. In Acts 1, he continues the story and explains why. In verse 8, he says they would become witnesses. Witnessing is not so much something we do with our mouth; rather it is the result of seeing with our eyes. When someone says they were an eyewitness to something, it means they observed it with their eyes. Then they told what they saw.

One of the most credible forms of testimony is eyewitness testimony. The person testifying has seen something and are willing to describe what they saw. As we use the eyes of our heart and observe what is reality in Heaven, that heavenly reality will collapse and change form into the thing needed. At that point our eyewitness testimony is two-fold. We have seen in Heaven, *and* now we see on the earth.

When I very recently learned much of this from Bible teacher Charity Kayembe in a video[30], I saw how it could impact everything we do and everything we understand about The Glory! Within the Glory is the unlimited potential of everything ever needed on the earth. It is the energy that can be transformed by observing with our spiritual eyes and seeing what God sees and agreeing with that. The Glory is limitless!

Jesus understood this when he stated:

All things have been delivered to Me by My Father, *and no one knows the Son except the Father. Nor does anyone know the Father except the Son, and the one to whom the Son wills to reveal Him. (Matthew 11:27) (Emphasis mine)*

As we assimilate these concepts (which will be easier to understand from the realms of Heaven), our lives will change, and situations will change—this applies to *every* arena!

---

[30] *Hearing God Through Your Dreams – Session 1 – Bridges to the Supernatural,* Charity Kayembe, Communion with God Ministries.

Chapter 10
In Conclusion

As you have journeyed through this book, it is our prayer that your ability to see in the spirit is unlocked now. At the very least, we pray that it much improved from when you started the book. We have seen dozens of people go from spiritual blindness to clarity in their spiritual seeing. If you have gotten this far and have not experienced improvement, please contact us. Do not give up! We won't!

This book is the second in our Engaging Heaven series. The first is called, *Cooperating with The Glory*. What I've been talking about, concerning the spiritual lien involves the Court of Titles and Deeds. I wrote a book on this court called, *Engaging the Courts for Ownership and Order*. It talks about getting false titles and false liens removed from your life so that you can make the progress that you need to do to make in the realm of the spirit.

Please contact us if you need a personal advocacy session where we assist people in the realms of the

Courts of Heaven, getting things unlocked that they have been unable to. You can schedule a Personal Advocacy Session at our website (www.courtsofheaven.net). We also work with ministries and businesses in this regard.

We also invite you to visit our website to review the resources available, including videos, process charts, prayer resources, and more so you can learn about the Courts of Heaven. We want to you learn how to operate in the Courts of Heaven and become proficient at setting yourself, your family, and your friends, and loved ones free, AND so that we can impact the nations via the Courts of Heaven.

Happy seeing!

Appendix A

Accessing the Realms of Heaven

This segment is from Engaging the Mercy Court of Heaven *and will help you learn to engage the realms of Heaven in a fresh way.*

A tremendous privilege we share in this time in history is the ability to access the realms of Heaven with ease. Many of us were taught that Heaven is only for after you die. Heaven is much more than a final destination on a journey, but also can be a vital aspect of that journey.

What I am about to share is vital in progressing in the various Courts of Heaven. We can access the Mercy Court while fully planted here on the earth, but to maximize our endeavors in the Courts of Heaven, we need to learn how to operate FROM Heaven.

In teaching on accessing the realms of Heaven, I often point out some simple facts. If you were to tell me you were a citizen of a particular town, but you could tell me little of it from your personal experience, I would tend to doubt the authenticity of your citizenship. I am a citizen of a small town in central North Carolina. I am familiar with the location of the city hall, police station, hospital, local county courthouse, Sheriff's Department, and much more. I know where many sporting events occur. I know where the parks are. I know many of the stores and restaurants. I am familiar with this small town. If I were to ask the average believer what they can describe of Heaven from personal experience, the answer will likely be nothing. They have no personal experience of Heaven that they can relate to me. It does not have to be like that.

In Matthew 3, Jesus informed us that the Kingdom of Heaven was at hand. You could say, "the Kingdom of Heaven is as close as your hand." Hold your hand up in front of your nose as close as you could. Do not touch your nose. Heaven is closer to you than that. It is not far, far away up in the sky. It is not "over yonder" as some old hymns describe. It is a very present reality separated from us by a very thin membrane – and we can access it by faith. It is very simple.

When Jesus was baptized in the River Jordan, as he came up out of the water IMMEDIATELY, the heavens were opened. He both saw (a dove) and heard (a voice coming from Heaven). This one act of Jesus restored our ability to access Heaven. We can experience open heavens over our life. We don't have to wait. We can live conscious of the realm of Heaven and live out of that reality!

Everything we do as believers we must do by faith. Accessing the realms of Heaven is done the same way. In Chapter 5, I spoke of how prophetic acts can create realities for us. It is the same with this. You can visualize stepping from one room into another easily. It is like stepping from one place to another. To learn to access the realms of Heaven, you will follow the same pattern.

Stand up from where you are now and prepare to work with me. You can experience the realms of Heaven right now! You don't have to wait until you are dressed up in a long box at the local funeral home or decorating an urn. You can experience Heaven while you are alive! Remember, we enter the Kingdom as a child.

Quiet yourself down. Turn off distracting background noises if possible. Prepare to relax and focus. Now, say this with me:

Father, I would like to access the realms of Heaven today, so right now, by faith, I take a step into the realms of Heaven. [As you say that, take a step forward.] Imagine you are going from one place to another in a single step. Once you have done so, pay attention to what you see and hear. You may see very bright lights; you may see a river, a pastoral scene, a garden – any number of things. You right now are experiencing a taste of Heaven. You will notice the peace that pervades the atmosphere of Heaven. You might notice the air seems electric with life. The testimonies I've heard are always amazing and beautiful to hear.

Now spend a few minutes in this place. Remember, Jesus said that to enter the Kingdom, you must come as a little child. I often coach people to imagine yourself as an 8-year-old with what you are seeing. What would an 8-year-old do? He or she would be inquisitive and ask, "What is this? What does that do? Where does that go? Can I go here?" If a child saw a river or a lake, what would that child want to do? Most would want to jump in the water.

The variety is infinite. The colors–amazing! The sounds are so beautiful. You can learn to do this regularly. When you access the realms of Heaven, you are home. You were made to experience the beauty that is Heaven.

The reason learning to access the realms of Heaven is crucial to engaging the Courts of Heaven is that much of what we do we do FROM Heaven. We need to learn to engage Heaven and work from it.

Many people tell me they can't "see" visually in the spirit. Often, they are discounting the ability they do have. They may be discounting their "knower." Every believer has a "knower" at work within them. This "knower" who is Holy Spirit at work within you helps you perceive things. Whether something is good or evil, He works to guide you more than you may have realized. Most navies that have submarines have a device known as sonar. Sonar gives a submarine "eyes" to see what is in their vicinity. They can detect what the object is by the ping emitted by the sonar. They can determine the distance to the object and if it is another submarine. They can even identify what class of submarine it might be. Sonar is invaluable in this setting, but a video camera would be rather useless underwater.

The military has a similar device for above ground situations known as radar. It functions in much the same manner. If a pilot were flying through thick cloud cover, the pilot would need to know what is in his path. Radar becomes his eyes.

Some people function visually. They often see what amounts to pictures or video images when they "see" in the spirit. They may see more detail. One operating by his or her "knower" (their spiritual radar or sonar) can be just as effective as a seer. If you operate more like sonar or radar, don't discount what you "see" in that manner. It is how I function, and I have been doing this type of work for many years.

I can often detect where an angel is in the room (or if it is one of the men or women in white linen and not an angel). I can often detect how many are present and whether they have something they are to give to someone. I can detect any number of things, and even though it is not "visual," it is still "seeing." It will set your

v

mind at ease when you understand that operating by your knower is just as valid as any other type of vision. It will help you to realize you have seen much more than you know and you may know much more than some who only see.

Courts Mentioned

Court of Appeals..30, 31, 32

Court of Cancellations 30, 34, 35, 36, 45, 46, 48, 50, 51

Courts of Healing 46

Court of Titles and Deeds...................... 4, 5, 40, 41, 43, 67

Mercy Court.. 28, 30, A1

Process Charts

Obstacles to Seeing Master X

Accusations XII

False Verdicts XIV

Covenants or Oaths XVI

Covenant of Death Release XVIII

Ownership Claims – Liens XX

Ownership Claims - False Titles XXII

Ownership Claims – Notes XXIV

Ownership Claims – Leases XXVI

Curses XXVIII

Generational Iniquities XXX

Invaders XXXIII

Trophy Room Release XXXIV

Regions of Captivity Release XXXVI

Release from Fear XXXVII

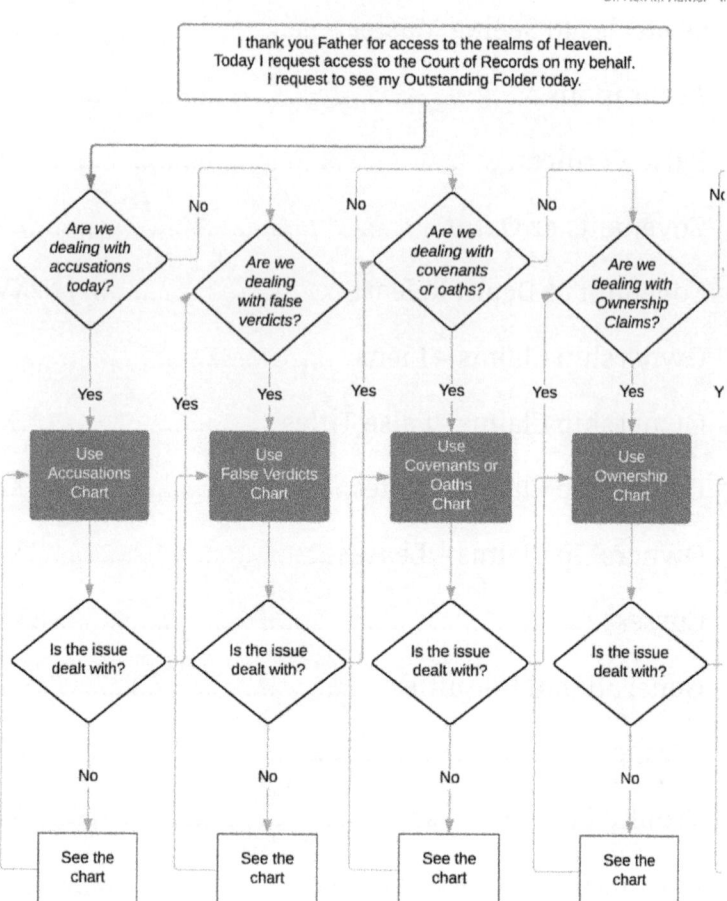

Obstacles

Dr. Ron M. Horner

```
I thank you Father for access to the realms of Heaven.
Today I request access to the Court of Records on my behalf.
I request to see my Outstanding Folder today.
```

- Are we dealing with accusations today? — **No** →
  - **Yes** → Use Accusations Chart → Is the issue dealt with? — **No** → See the chart
- Are we dealing with false verdicts? — **No** →
  - **Yes** → Use False Verdicts Chart → Is the issue dealt with? — **No** → See the chart
- Are we dealing with covenants or oaths? — **No** →
  - **Yes** → Use Covenants or Oaths Chart → Is the issue dealt with? — **No** → See the chart
- Are we dealing with Ownership Claims? — **No** →
  - **Yes** → Use Ownership Chart → Is the issue dealt with? — **No** → See the chart

Copyright ©2019 Dr. Ron M. Horner | www.courtsofheaven.net | Use by permission

x

to Seeing

www.courtsofheaven.net

> If you are having trouble seeing or reading your folder, simply ask questions you can get a yes or no answer to.

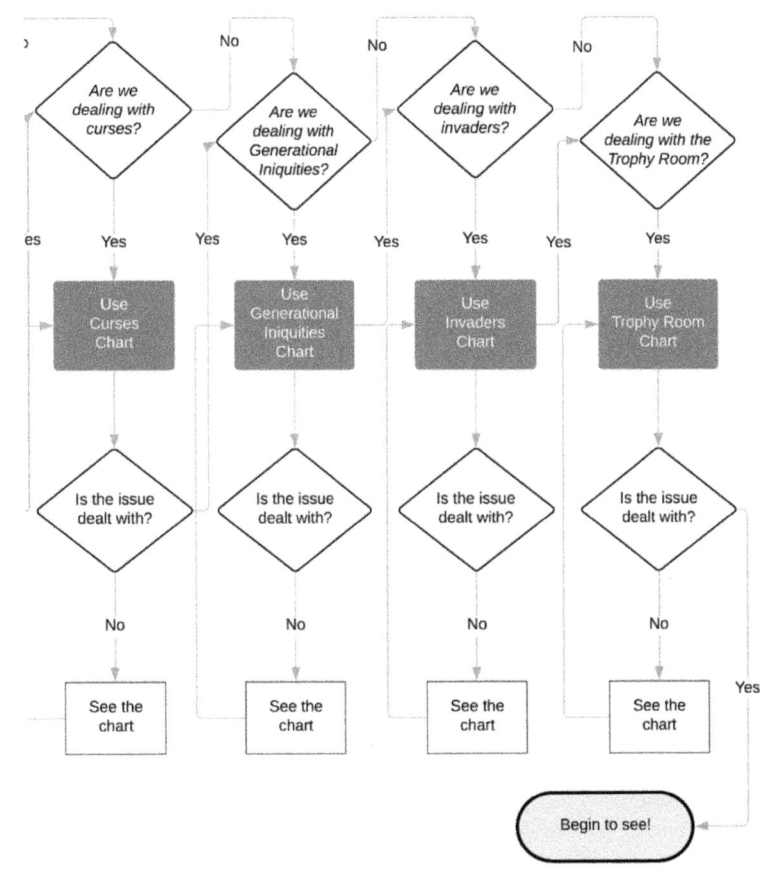

```
          No                No                  No
    ┌─────────┐      ┌─────────────┐     ┌─────────┐      ┌──────────────┐
    │ Are we  │      │   Are we    │     │ Are we  │      │   Are we     │
    │dealing  │      │ dealing with│     │dealing  │      │ dealing with │
    │with     │      │Generational │     │with     │      │  the Trophy  │
    │curses?  │      │ Iniquities? │     │invaders?│      │    Room?     │
    └─────────┘      └─────────────┘     └─────────┘      └──────────────┘
       Yes               Yes                Yes               Yes
        ▼                 ▼                  ▼                 ▼
    ┌────────┐       ┌──────────────┐    ┌─────────┐      ┌──────────────┐
    │  Use   │       │     Use      │    │   Use   │      │     Use      │
    │ Curses │       │ Generational │    │ Invaders│      │ Trophy Room  │
    │ Chart  │       │  Iniquities  │    │  Chart  │      │    Chart     │
    │        │       │    Chart     │    │         │      │              │
    └────────┘       └──────────────┘    └─────────┘      └──────────────┘
        ▼                 ▼                  ▼                 ▼
    ┌─────────┐      ┌─────────┐        ┌─────────┐       ┌─────────┐
    │Is the   │      │Is the   │        │Is the   │       │Is the   │
    │issue    │      │issue    │        │issue    │       │issue    │
    │dealt    │      │dealt    │        │dealt    │       │dealt    │
    │with?    │      │with?    │        │with?    │       │with?    │
    └─────────┘      └─────────┘        └─────────┘       └─────────┘
        No               No                 No                No
        ▼                ▼                  ▼                 ▼                Yes
    ┌────────┐       ┌────────┐         ┌────────┐        ┌────────┐
    │See the │       │See the │         │See the │        │See the │
    │ chart  │       │ chart  │         │ chart  │        │ chart  │
    └────────┘       └────────┘         └────────┘        └────────┘
                                              ( Begin to see! )
```

None of the processes offered here constitute medical or legal advice. The focus is spiritual direction.

Obstacles to Seeing

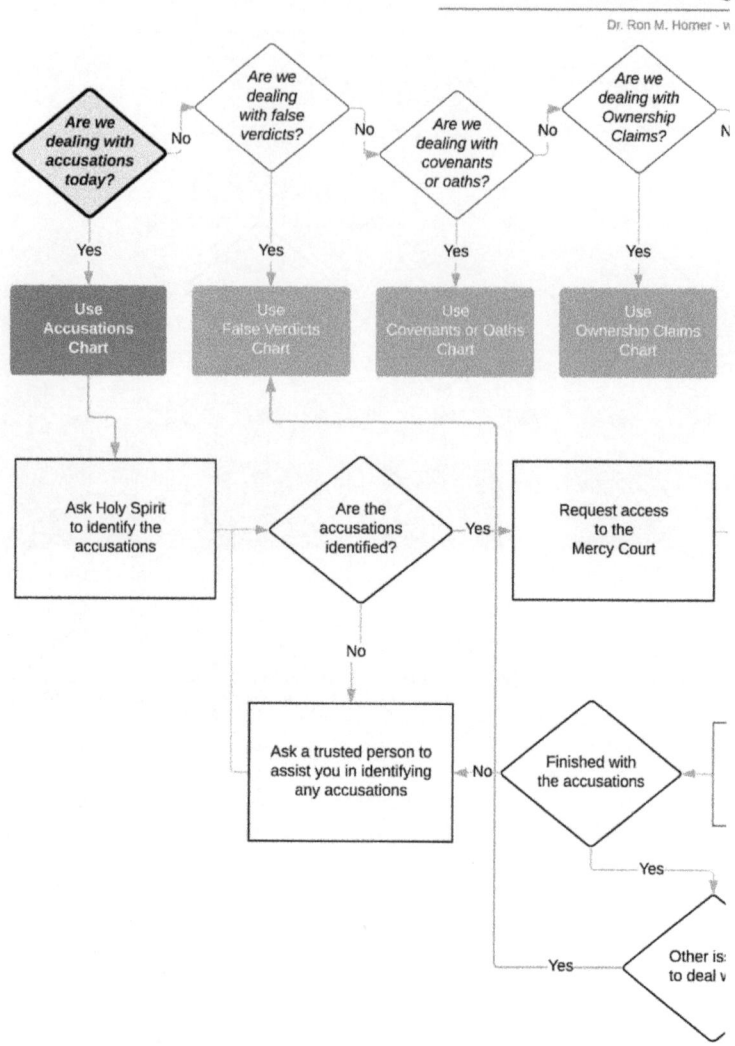

Dr. Ron M. Horner - w

- **Are we dealing with accusations today?** — No → **Are we dealing with false verdicts?** — No → **Are we dealing with covenants or oaths?** — No → **Are we dealing with Ownership Claims?** — N
  - Yes → Use Accusations Chart
  - Yes → Use False Verdicts Chart
  - Yes → Use Covenants or Oaths Chart
  - Yes → Use Ownership Claims Chart

Use Accusations Chart → Ask Holy Spirit to identify the accusations → **Are the accusations identified?**
- Yes → Request access to the Mercy Court
- No → Ask a trusted person to assist you in identifying any accusations → No → **Finished with the accusations**
  - Yes → Other iss: to deal v
  - Yes →

Copyright ©2019 Dr. Ron M. Horner | www.courtsofheaven.net | Use by permission

I - Accusations Chart

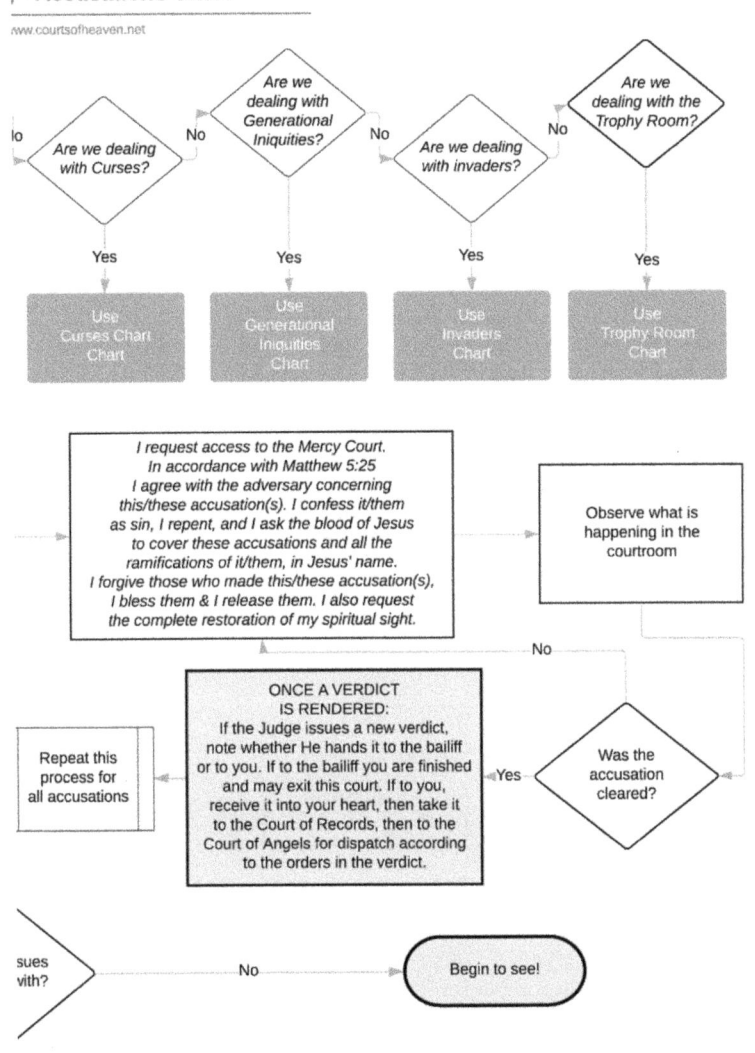

www.courtsofheaven.net

Are we dealing with Curses? — No → Are we dealing with Generational Iniquities? — No → Are we dealing with invaders? — No → Are we dealing with the Trophy Room?

- Yes → Use Curses Chart Chart
- Yes → Use Generational Iniquities Chart
- Yes → Use Invaders Chart
- Yes → Use Trophy Room Chart

I request access to the Mercy Court.
In accordance with Matthew 5:25 I agree with the adversary concerning this/these accusation(s). I confess it/them as sin, I repent, and I ask the blood of Jesus to cover these accusations and all the ramifications of it/them, in Jesus' name. I forgive those who made this/these accusation(s), I bless them & I release them. I also request the complete restoration of my spiritual sight.

→ Observe what is happening in the courtroom

ONCE A VERDICT IS RENDERED:
If the Judge issues a new verdict, note whether He hands it to the bailiff or to you. If to the bailiff you are finished and may exit this court. If to you, receive it into your heart, then take it to the Court of Records, then to the Court of Angels for dispatch according to the orders in the verdict.

Was the accusation cleared?
- Yes → Repeat this process for all accusations
- No → (back to verdict box)

sues with? — No → Begin to see!

None of the processes offered here constitute medical or legal advice. The focus is spiritual direction.

XIII

Obstacles to Seeing

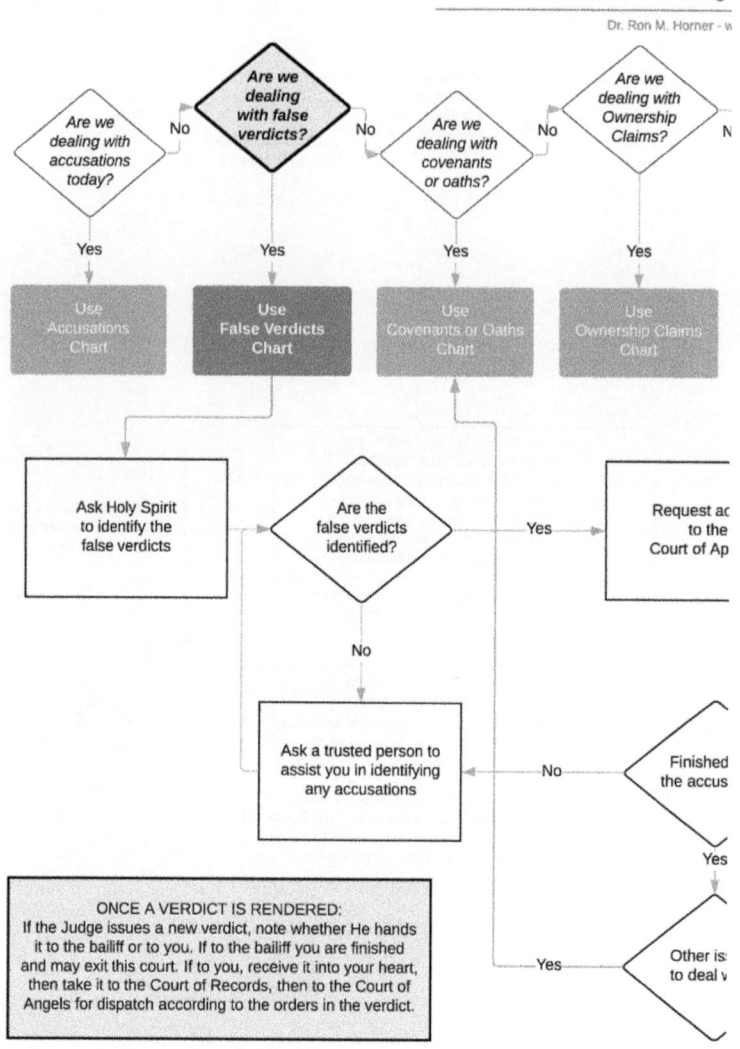

Dr. Ron M. Horner - w

- Are we dealing with accusations today? — No →
- Are we dealing with false verdicts? — No →
- Are we dealing with covenants or oaths? — No →
- Are we dealing with Ownership Claims? — N

Yes ↓ Use Accusations Chart

Yes ↓ Use False Verdicts Chart

Yes ↓ Use Covenants or Oaths Chart

Yes ↓ Use Ownership Claims Chart

Ask Holy Spirit to identify the false verdicts

Are the false verdicts identified? — Yes → Request ac to the Court of Ap

No ↓

Ask a trusted person to assist you in identifying any accusations ← No — Finished the accus

Yes ↓

— Yes → Other is: to deal v

ONCE A VERDICT IS RENDERED:
If the Judge issues a new verdict, note whether He hands it to the bailiff or to you. If to the bailiff you are finished and may exit this court. If to you, receive it into your heart, then take it to the Court of Records, then to the Court of Angels for dispatch according to the orders in the verdict.

Copyright ©2019 Dr. Ron M. Horner | www.courtsofheaven.net | Use by permission

- False Verdicts Chart
www.courtsofheaven.net

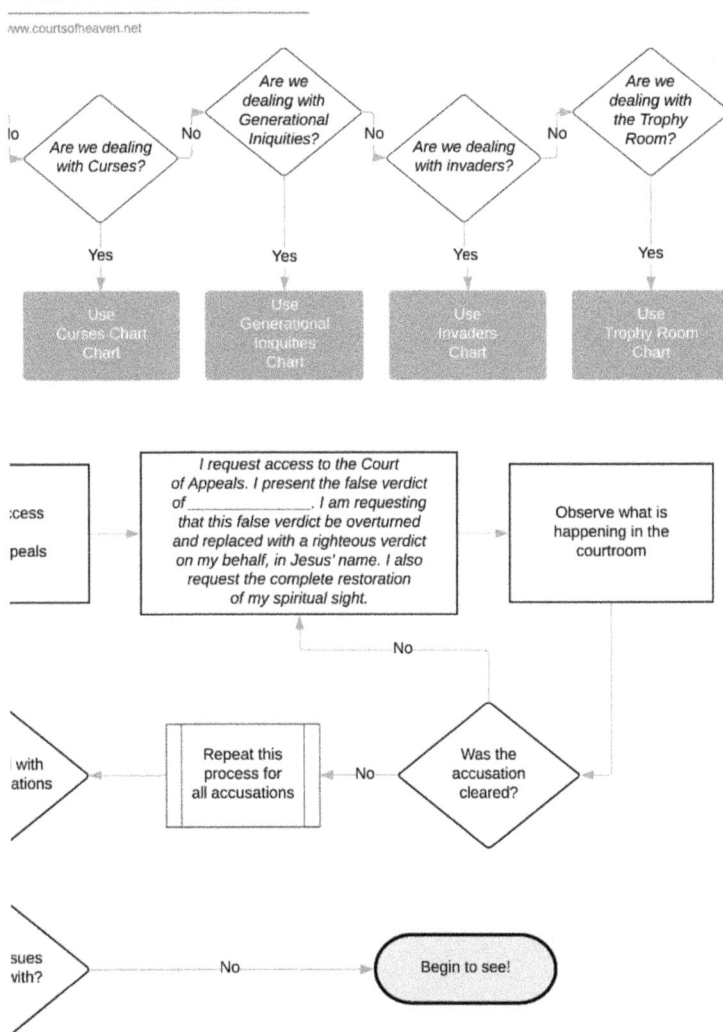

- Are we dealing with Curses? — **Yes** → Use Curses Chart Chart
- **No** → Are we dealing with Generational Iniquities? — **Yes** → Use Generational Iniquities Chart
- **No** → Are we dealing with invaders? — **Yes** → Use Invaders Chart
- **No** → Are we dealing with the Trophy Room? — **Yes** → Use Trophy Room Chart

> I request access to the Court of Appeals. I present the false verdict of _____. I am requesting that this false verdict be overturned and replaced with a righteous verdict on my behalf, in Jesus' name. I also request the complete restoration of my spiritual sight.

→ Observe what is happening in the courtroom

→ Was the accusation cleared? — **No** → Repeat this process for all accusations (loop back)

— **No** → Begin to see!

None of the processes offered here constitute medical or legal advice. The focus is spiritual direction.

XV

Obstacles to Seeing - C

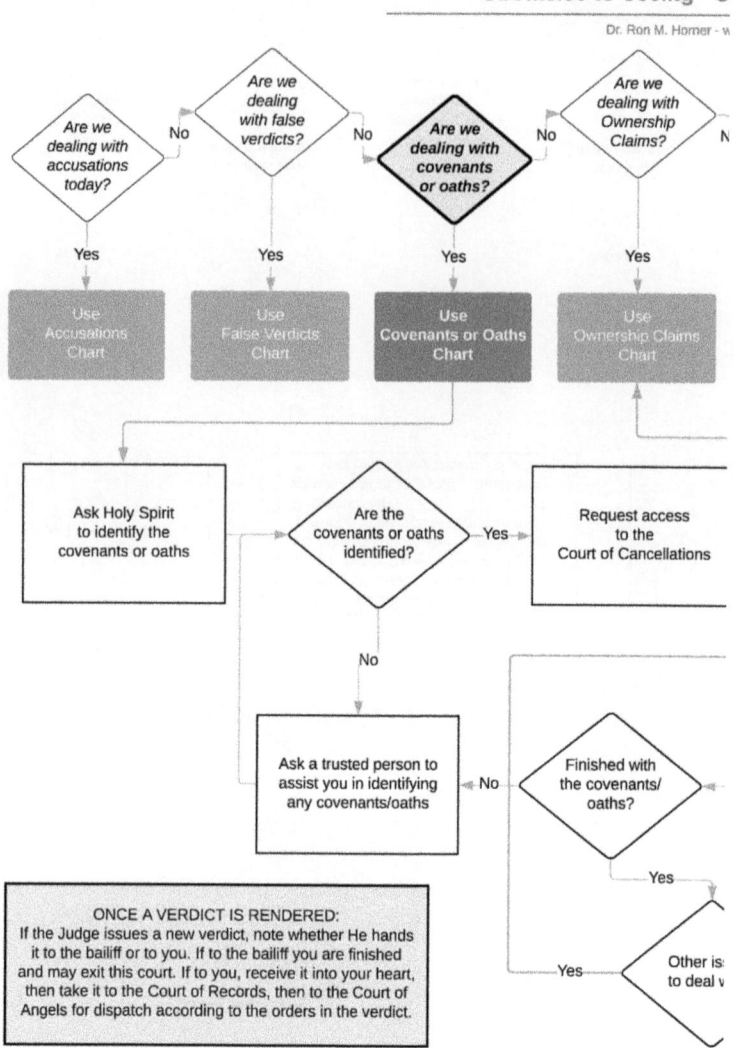

Dr. Ron M. Horner

```
                                    ┌──────────────┐
                                    │  Are we      │
                    ┌──────────┐    │  dealing     │    ┌──────────┐              ┌──────────┐
    ┌──────────┐    │ Are we   │    │  with false  │    │ Are we   │              │ Are we   │
    │ Are we   │    │ dealing  │    │  verdicts?   │    │ dealing  │              │ dealing  │
    │ dealing  │─No→│ with     │─No→│              │─No→│ with     │─No→          │ with     │
    │ with     │    │ false    │    │              │    │covenants │              │Ownership │
    │accusations│   │verdicts? │    │              │    │or oaths? │              │ Claims?  │
    │  today?  │    └──────────┘    └──────────────┘    └──────────┘              └──────────┘
    └──────────┘         │                 │                 │                          │
         │              Yes               Yes               Yes                        Yes
        Yes              ↓                 ↓                 ↓                          ↓
         ↓          ┌─────────┐      ┌─────────┐       ┌──────────┐              ┌──────────┐
    ┌─────────┐     │  Use    │      │  Use    │       │   Use    │              │   Use    │
    │  Use    │     │ False   │      │Covenants│       │Covenants │              │Ownership │
    │Accusations│   │Verdicts │      │or Oaths │       │ or Oaths │              │  Claims  │
    │  Chart  │     │ Chart   │      │ Chart   │       │  Chart   │              │  Chart   │
    └─────────┘     └─────────┘      └─────────┘       └──────────┘              └──────────┘
```

Ask Holy Spirit to identify the covenants or oaths → **Are the covenants or oaths identified?** —Yes→ **Request access to the Court of Cancellations**

↓ No

Ask a trusted person to assist you in identifying any covenants/oaths ←No— **Finished with the covenants/oaths?**

—Yes→

—Yes→ Other is... to deal...

ONCE A VERDICT IS RENDERED:
If the Judge issues a new verdict, note whether He hands it to the bailiff or to you. If to the bailiff you are finished and may exit this court. If to you, receive it into your heart, then take it to the Court of Records, then to the Court of Angels for dispatch according to the orders in the verdict.

Copyright ©2019 Dr. Ron M. Horner | www.courtsofheaven.net | Use by permission

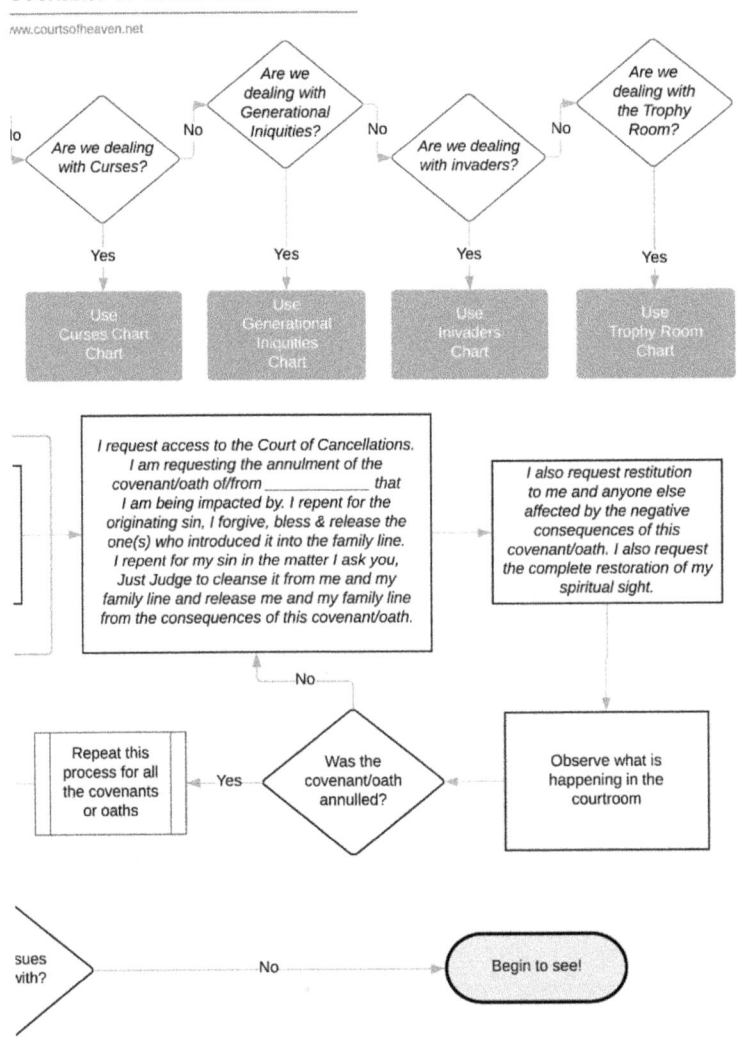

ovenants or Oaths Chart

www.courtsofheaven.net

```
                    Are we                                              Are we
                    dealing with                                        dealing with
                    Generational          Are we dealing                the Trophy
   Are we dealing   Iniquities?           with invaders?                Room?
   with Curses?
```

Yes	Yes	Yes	Yes
Use Curses Chart	Use Generational Iniquities Chart	Use Invaders Chart	Use Trophy Room Chart

I request access to the Court of Cancellations. I am requesting the annulment of the covenant/oath of/from _____ that I am being impacted by. I repent for the originating sin, I forgive, bless & release the one(s) who introduced it into the family line. I repent for my sin in the matter I ask you, Just Judge to cleanse it from me and my family line and release me and my family line from the consequences of this covenant/oath.

I also request restitution to me and anyone else affected by the negative consequences of this covenant/oath. I also request the complete restoration of my spiritual sight.

— No —

Was the covenant/oath annulled?

— Yes → **Repeat this process for all the covenants or oaths**

Observe what is happening in the courtroom

sues vith? — No → **Begin to see!**

None of the processes offered here constitute medical or legal advice. The focus is spiritual direction.

XVII

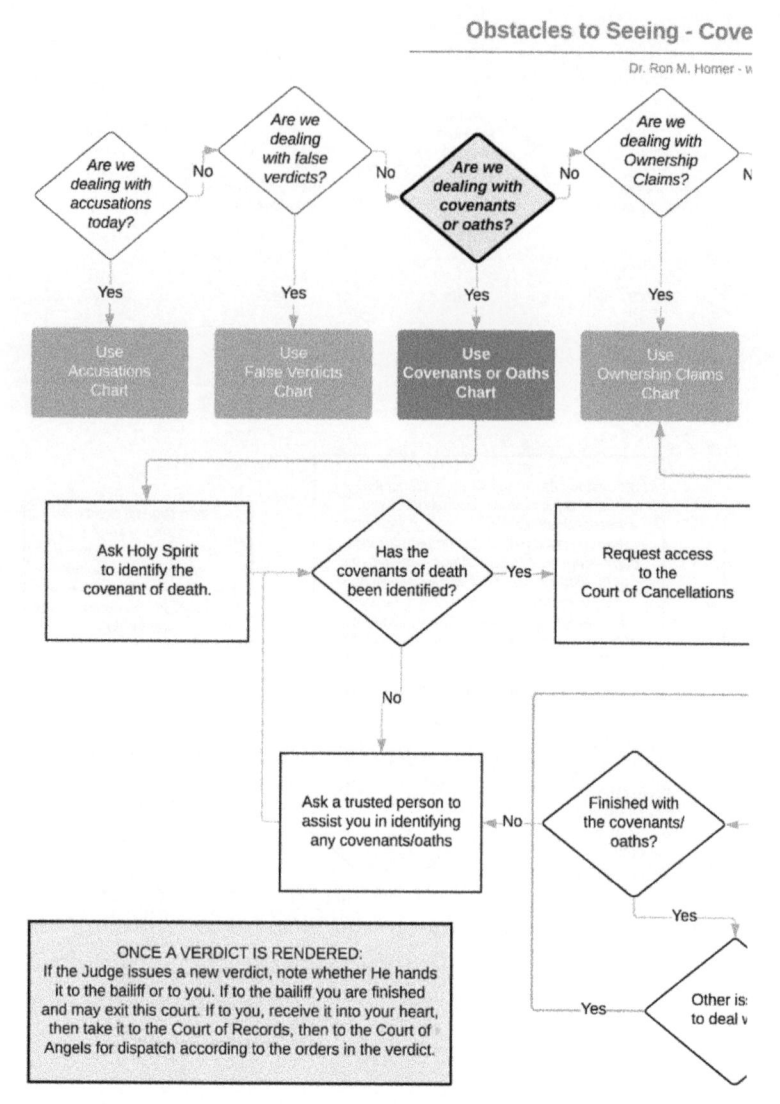

Obstacles to Seeing - Cove

Dr. Ron M. Horner

```
                  Are we                            Are we
                 dealing                           dealing
   Are we       with false       Are we            with
  dealing    No  verdicts?   No  dealing with  No  Ownership   N
  with                           covenants         Claims?
  accusations                    or oaths?
  today?

    Yes           Yes             Yes             Yes

    Use           Use             Use             Use
 Accusations  False Verdicts  Covenants or Oaths  Ownership Claims
    Chart        Chart           Chart            Chart
```

Ask Holy Spirit to identify the covenant of death.

Has the covenants of death been identified? — Yes → Request access to the Court of Cancellations

No

Ask a trusted person to assist you in identifying any covenants/oaths ← No — Finished with the covenants/oaths?

Yes

Other is to deal v

Yes

ONCE A VERDICT IS RENDERED:
If the Judge issues a new verdict, note whether He hands it to the bailiff or to you. If to the bailiff you are finished and may exit this court. If to you, receive it into your heart, then take it to the Court of Records, then to the Court of Angels for dispatch according to the orders in the verdict.

Copyright ©2019 Dr. Ron M. Horner | www.courtsofheaven.net | Use by permission

XVIII

nant of Death Release Chart

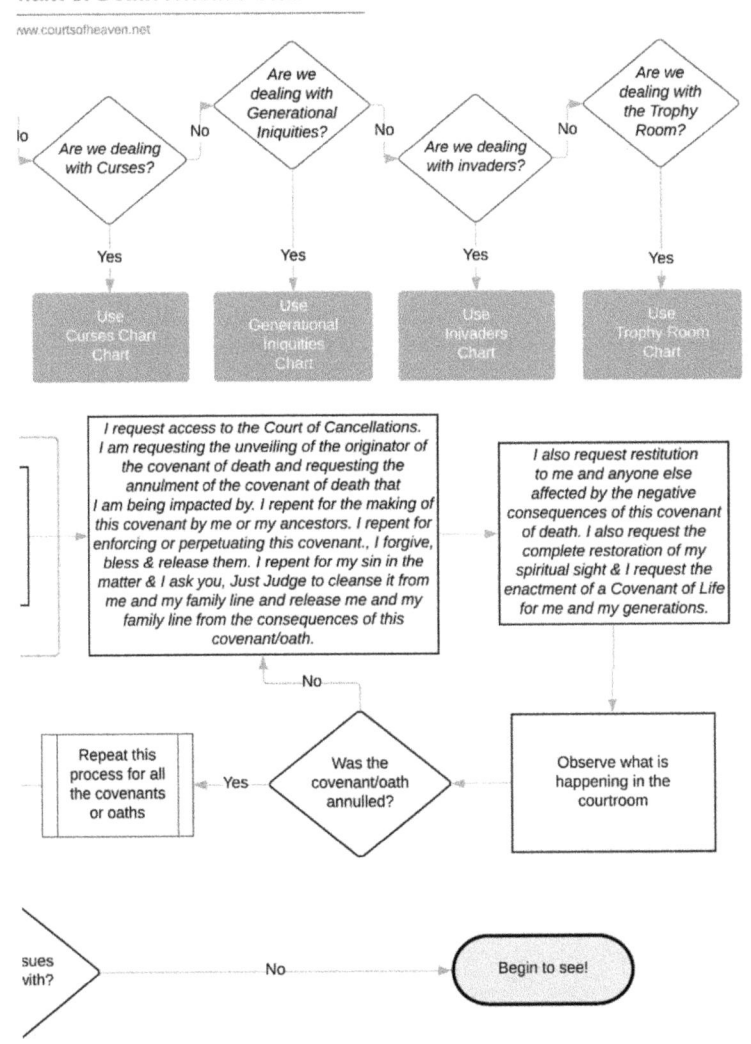

www.courtsofheaven.net

```
                    Are we                                              Are we
                    dealing with                                        dealing with
                    Generational                                        the Trophy
     No             Iniquities?          No                      No     Room?
Are we dealing                                Are we dealing
with Curses?                                  with invaders?

    Yes                 Yes                      Yes                       Yes

   Use                  Use                      Use                      Use
Curses Chart        Generational              Invaders                Trophy Room
   Chart             Iniquities                 Chart                    Chart
                       Chart
```

I request access to the Court of Cancellations. I am requesting the unveiling of the originator of the covenant of death and requesting the annulment of the covenant of death that I am being impacted by. I repent for the making of this covenant by me or my ancestors. I repent for enforcing or perpetuating this covenant., I forgive, bless & release them. I repent for my sin in the matter & I ask you, Just Judge to cleanse it from me and my family line and release me and my family line from the consequences of this covenant/oath.

I also request restitution to me and anyone else affected by the negative consequences of this covenant of death. I also request the complete restoration of my spiritual sight & I request the enactment of a Covenant of Life for me and my generations.

— No —

| Repeat this process for all the covenants or oaths | ← Yes — | Was the covenant/oath annulled? | → | Observe what is happening in the courtroom |

sues with? — No — → **Begin to see!**

None of the processes offered here constitute medical or legal advice. The focus is spiritual direction.

XIX

Obstacles to Seeing - Own

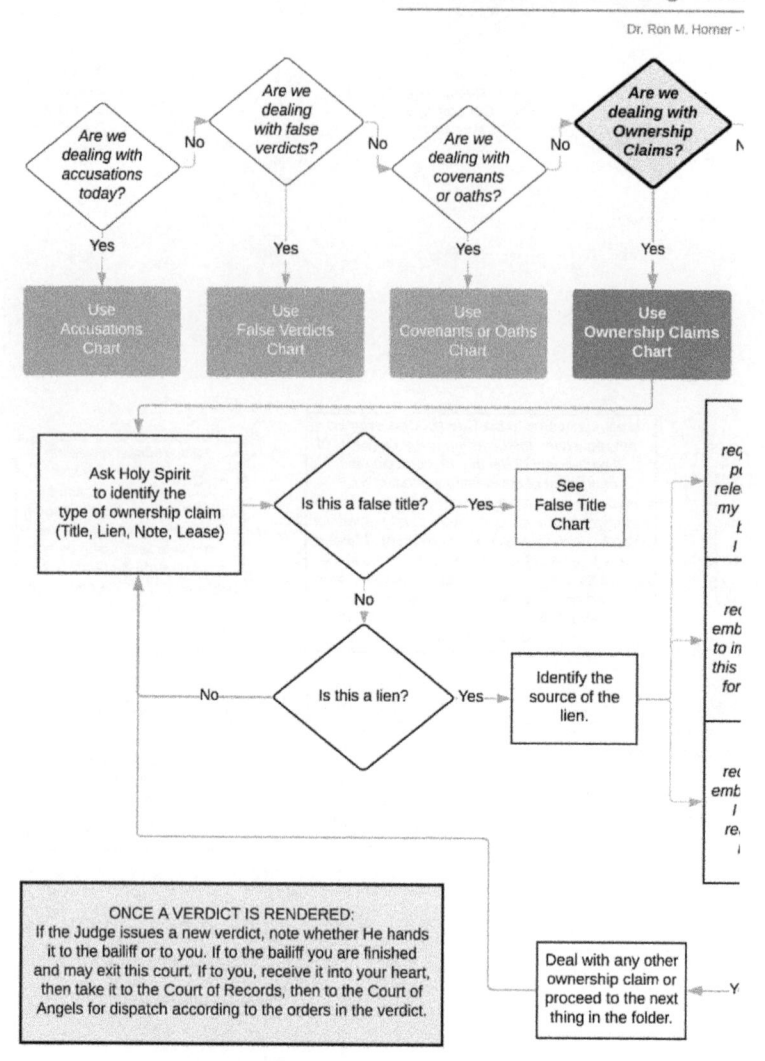

Dr. Ron M. Horner

```
Are we dealing with accusations today? ──No──► Are we dealing with false verdicts? ──No──► Are we dealing with covenants or oaths? ──No──► Are we dealing with Ownership Claims?
        │                                    │                                          │                                             │
       Yes                                  Yes                                        Yes                                           Yes
        ▼                                    ▼                                          ▼                                             ▼
   Use Accusations                    Use False Verdicts                      Use Covenants or Oaths                        Use Ownership Claims
       Chart                                Chart                                      Chart                                        Chart
```

Ask Holy Spirit to identify the type of ownership claim (Title, Lien, Note, Lease) → Is this a false title? —Yes→ See False Title Chart

↓ No

Is this a lien? —Yes→ Identify the source of the lien.

No →

ONCE A VERDICT IS RENDERED:
If the Judge issues a new verdict, note whether He hands it to the bailiff or to you. If to the bailiff you are finished and may exit this court. If to you, receive it into your heart, then take it to the Court of Records, then to the Court of Angels for dispatch according to the orders in the verdict.

Deal with any other ownership claim or proceed to the next thing in the folder.

Copyright ©2019 Dr. Ron M. Horner | www.courtsofheaven.net | Use by permission

...ership Claims Chart - Liens

www.courtsofheaven.net

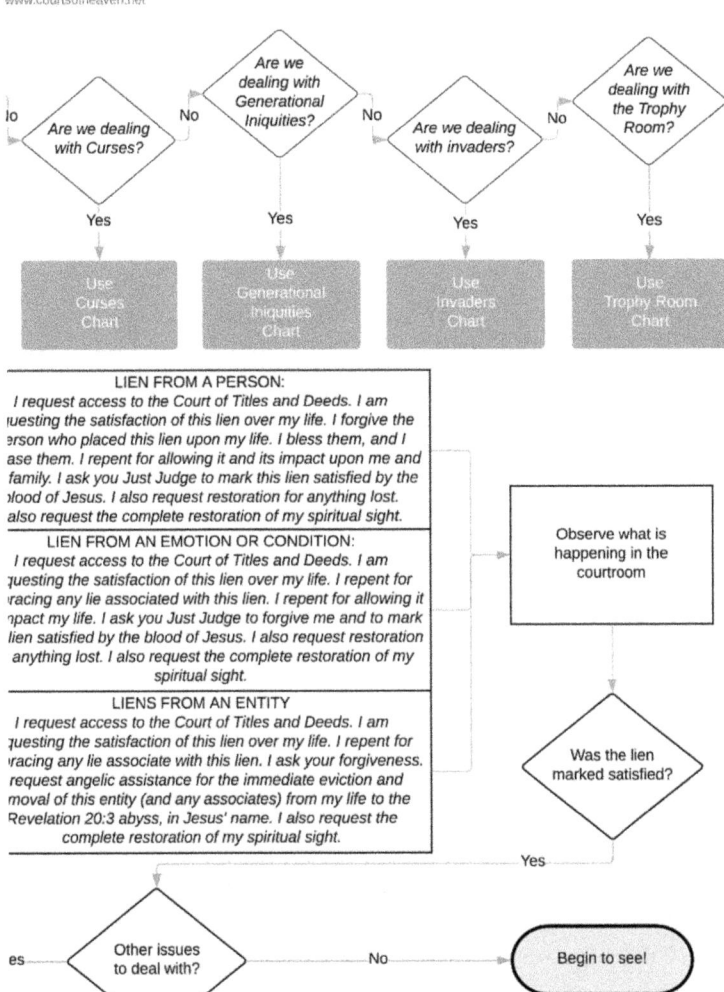

Decision flow (top row):
- Are we dealing with Curses? → No → Are we dealing with Generational Iniquities? → No → Are we dealing with invaders? → No → Are we dealing with the Trophy Room?
- Yes → Use Curses Chart
- Yes → Use Generational Iniquities Chart
- Yes → Use Invaders Chart
- Yes → Use Trophy Room Chart

LIEN FROM A PERSON:
I request access to the Court of Titles and Deeds. I am requesting the satisfaction of this lien over my life. I forgive the person who placed this lien upon my life. I bless them, and I release them. I repent for allowing it and its impact upon me and family. I ask you Just Judge to mark this lien satisfied by the blood of Jesus. I also request restoration for anything lost. I also request the complete restoration of my spiritual sight.

LIEN FROM AN EMOTION OR CONDITION:
I request access to the Court of Titles and Deeds. I am requesting the satisfaction of this lien over my life. I repent for embracing any lie associated with this lien. I repent for allowing it impact my life. I ask you Just Judge to forgive me and to mark lien satisfied by the blood of Jesus. I also request restoration anything lost. I also request the complete restoration of my spiritual sight.

LIENS FROM AN ENTITY:
I request access to the Court of Titles and Deeds. I am requesting the satisfaction of this lien over my life. I repent for embracing any lie associate with this lien. I ask your forgiveness. request angelic assistance for the immediate eviction and removal of this entity (and any associates) from my life to the Revelation 20:3 abyss, in Jesus' name. I also request the complete restoration of my spiritual sight.

Observe what is happening in the courtroom

Was the lien marked satisfied? → Yes →

Other issues to deal with? → Yes → (loop back) / No → Begin to see!

None of the processes offered here constitute medical or legal advice. The focus is spiritual direction.

Obstacles to Seeing - Ownership

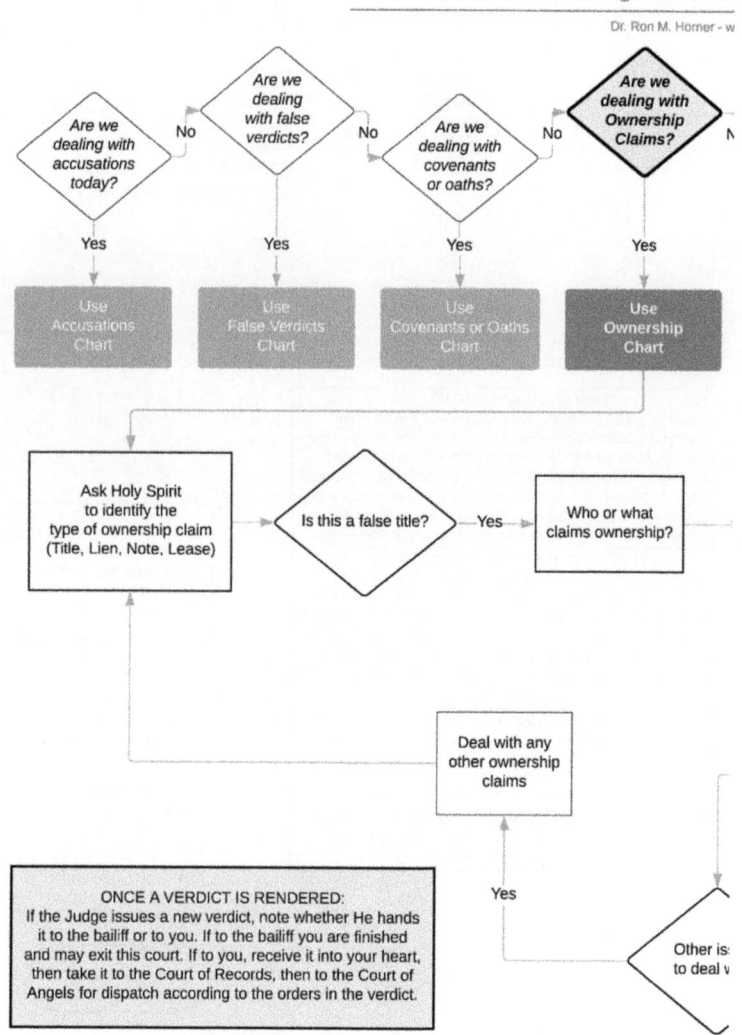

Dr. Ron M. Horner - w

- **Are we dealing with accusations today?** — No → **Are we dealing with false verdicts?** — No → **Are we dealing with covenants or oaths?** — No → **Are we dealing with Ownership Claims?** — N
  - Yes ↓ Use Accusations Chart
  - Yes ↓ Use False Verdicts Chart
  - Yes ↓ Use Covenants or Oaths Chart
  - Yes ↓ Use Ownership Chart

Ask Holy Spirit to identify the type of ownership claim (Title, Lien, Note, Lease) → Is this a false title? — Yes → Who or what claims ownership?

Deal with any other ownership claims

ONCE A VERDICT IS RENDERED:
If the Judge issues a new verdict, note whether He hands it to the bailiff or to you. If to the bailiff you are finished and may exit this court. If to you, receive it into your heart, then take it to the Court of Records, then to the Court of Angels for dispatch according to the orders in the verdict.

Yes

Other is: to deal v

Copyright ©2019 Dr. Ron M. Horner | www.courtsofheaven.net | Use by permission

hip Claims Chart - False Titles

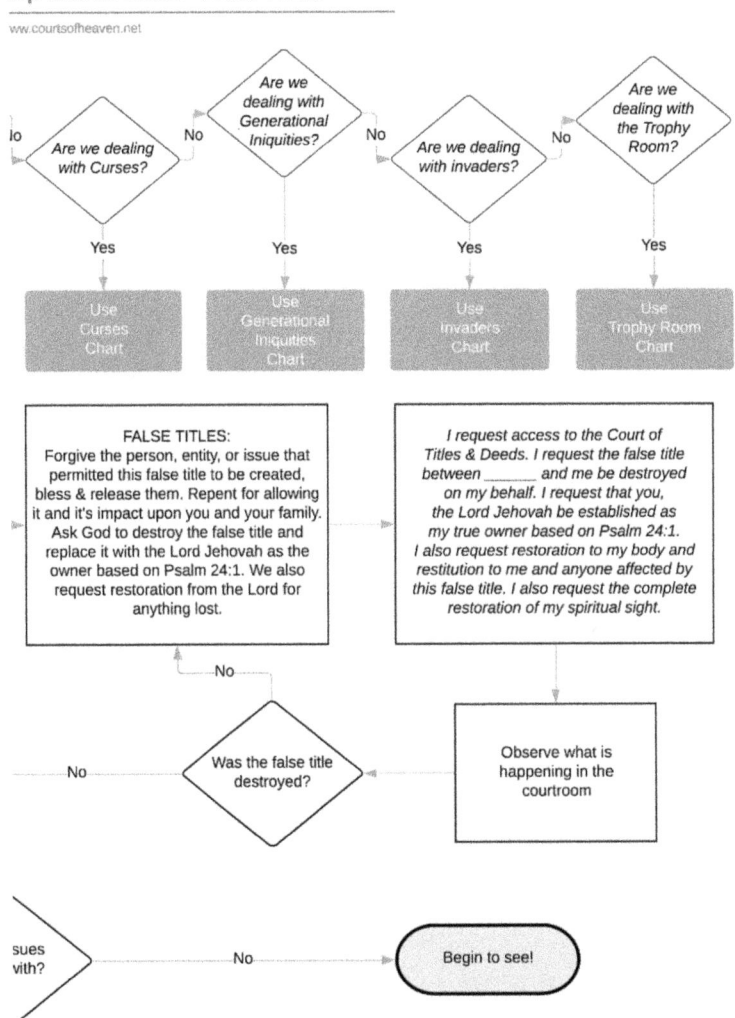

www.courtsofheaven.net

- Are we dealing with Curses? — Yes → **Use Curses Chart**
- Are we dealing with Generational Iniquities? — Yes → **Use Generational Iniquities Chart**
- Are we dealing with invaders? — Yes → **Use Invaders Chart**
- Are we dealing with the Trophy Room? — Yes → **Use Trophy Room Chart**

FALSE TITLES:
Forgive the person, entity, or issue that permitted this false title to be created, bless & release them. Repent for allowing it and it's impact upon you and your family. Ask God to destroy the false title and replace it with the Lord Jehovah as the owner based on Psalm 24:1. We also request restoration from the Lord for anything lost.

I request access to the Court of Titles & Deeds. I request the false title between _____ and me be destroyed on my behalf. I request that you, the Lord Jehovah be established as my true owner based on Psalm 24:1. I also request restoration to my body and restitution to me and anyone affected by this false title. I also request the complete restoration of my spiritual sight.

Was the false title destroyed? — No

Observe what is happening in the courtroom

— No → **Begin to see!**

None of the processes offered here constitute medical or legal advice. The focus is spiritual direction.

Obstacles to Seeing - Ownership

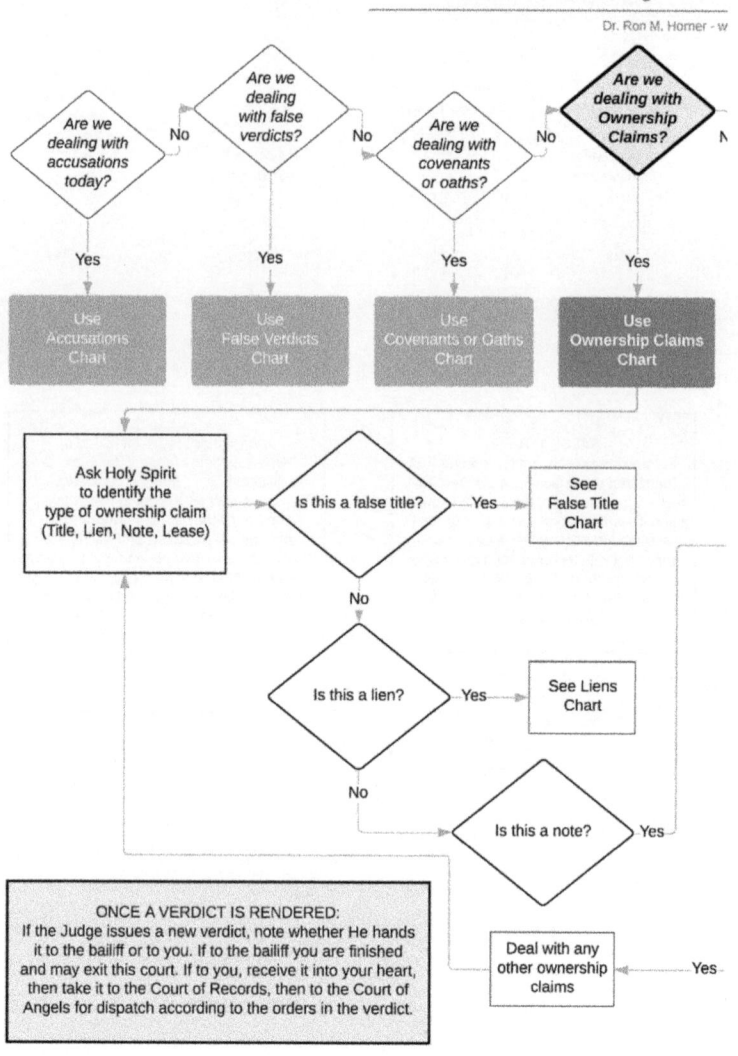

Dr. Ron M. Horner - w

- Are we dealing with accusations today? — No →
- Are we dealing with false verdicts? — No →
- Are we dealing with covenants or oaths? — No →
- Are we dealing with Ownership Claims? — Yes →

- Yes → Use Accusations Chart
- Yes → Use False Verdicts Chart
- Yes → Use Covenants or Oaths Chart
- Yes → Use Ownership Claims Chart

Ask Holy Spirit to identify the type of ownership claim (Title, Lien, Note, Lease)

- Is this a false title? — Yes → See False Title Chart
- No ↓
- Is this a lien? — Yes → See Liens Chart
- No ↓
- Is this a note? — Yes ↓
- Deal with any other ownership claims ← Yes

ONCE A VERDICT IS RENDERED:
If the Judge issues a new verdict, note whether He hands it to the bailiff or to you. If to the bailiff you are finished and may exit this court. If to you, receive it into your heart, then take it to the Court of Records, then to the Court of Angels for dispatch according to the orders in the verdict.

Copyright ©2019 Dr. Ron M. Horner | www.courtsofheaven.net | Use by permission

ership Claims Chart - Notes

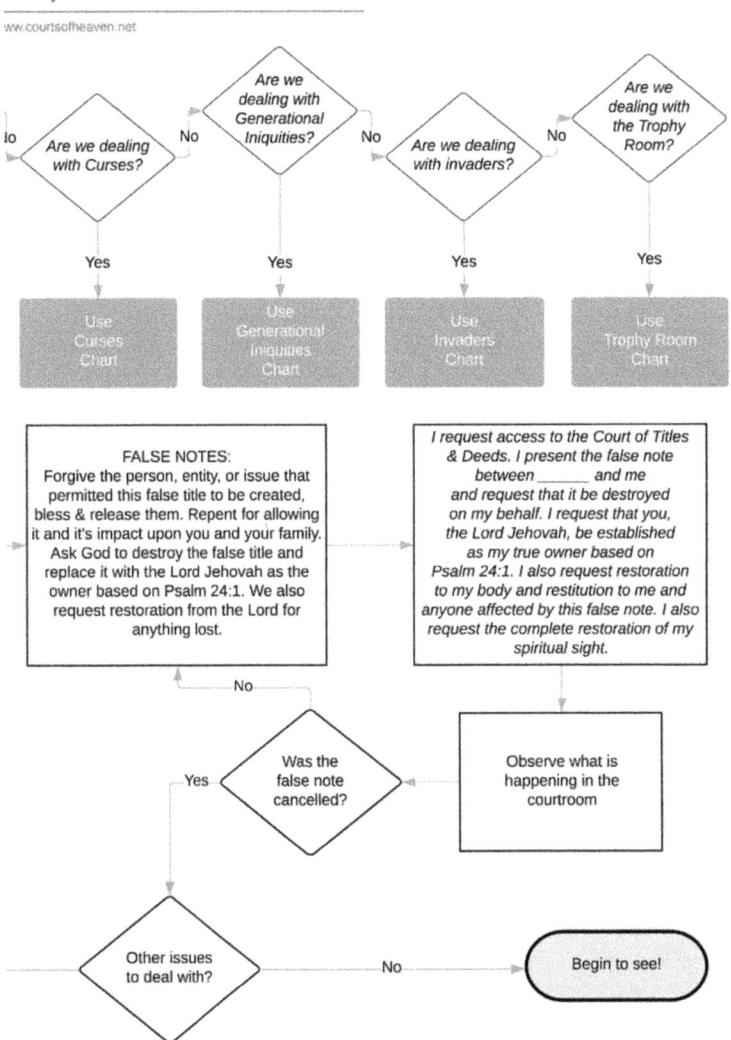

ww.courtsofheaven.net

Are we dealing with Curses? — No → **Are we dealing with Generational Iniquities?** — No → **Are we dealing with invaders?** — No → **Are we dealing with the Trophy Room?**

- Yes (Curses) → Use Curses Chart
- Yes (Generational Iniquities) → Use Generational Iniquities Chart
- Yes (Invaders) → Use Invaders Chart
- Yes (Trophy Room) → Use Trophy Room Chart

FALSE NOTES:
Forgive the person, entity, or issue that permitted this false title to be created, bless & release them. Repent for allowing it and it's impact upon you and your family. Ask God to destroy the false title and replace it with the Lord Jehovah as the owner based on Psalm 24:1. We also request restoration from the Lord for anything lost.

→ I request access to the Court of Titles & Deeds. I present the false note between _____ and me and request that it be destroyed on my behalf. I request that you, the Lord Jehovah, be established as my true owner based on Psalm 24:1. I also request restoration to my body and restitution to me and anyone affected by this false note. I also request the complete restoration of my spiritual sight.

Was the false note cancelled?
- Yes → Other issues to deal with? — No → **Begin to see!**
- No → Observe what is happening in the courtroom

None of the processes offered here constitute medical or legal advice. The focus is spiritual direction.

Obstacles to Seeing - Owne[rship]

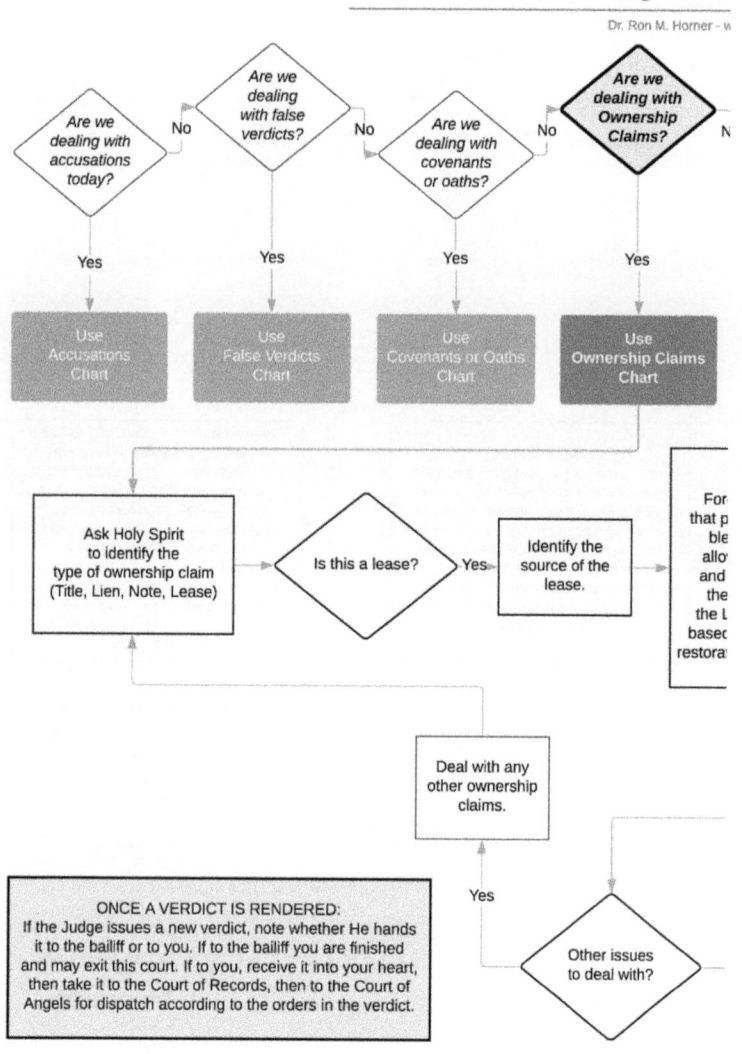

Dr. Ron M. Horner - w[...]

- Are we dealing with accusations today? — **No** →
- Are we dealing with false verdicts? — **No** →
- Are we dealing with covenants or oaths? — **No** →
- **Are we dealing with Ownership Claims?** — N[o]

Yes branches:
- Use Accusations Chart
- Use False Verdicts Chart
- Use Covenants or Oaths Chart
- Use Ownership Claims Chart

Ask Holy Spirit to identify the type of ownership claim (Title, Lien, Note, Lease) → Is this a lease? — **Yes** → Identify the source of the lease.

For [...] that p[...] ble [...] allo[w...] and [...] the [...] the L[...] based [...] restora[tion...]

Deal with any other ownership claims.

Yes → Other issues to deal with?

ONCE A VERDICT IS RENDERED:
If the Judge issues a new verdict, note whether He hands it to the bailiff or to you. If to the bailiff you are finished and may exit this court. If to you, receive it into your heart, then take it to the Court of Records, then to the Court of Angels for dispatch according to the orders in the verdict.

Copyright ©2019 Dr. Ron M. Horner | www.courtsofheaven.net | Use by permission

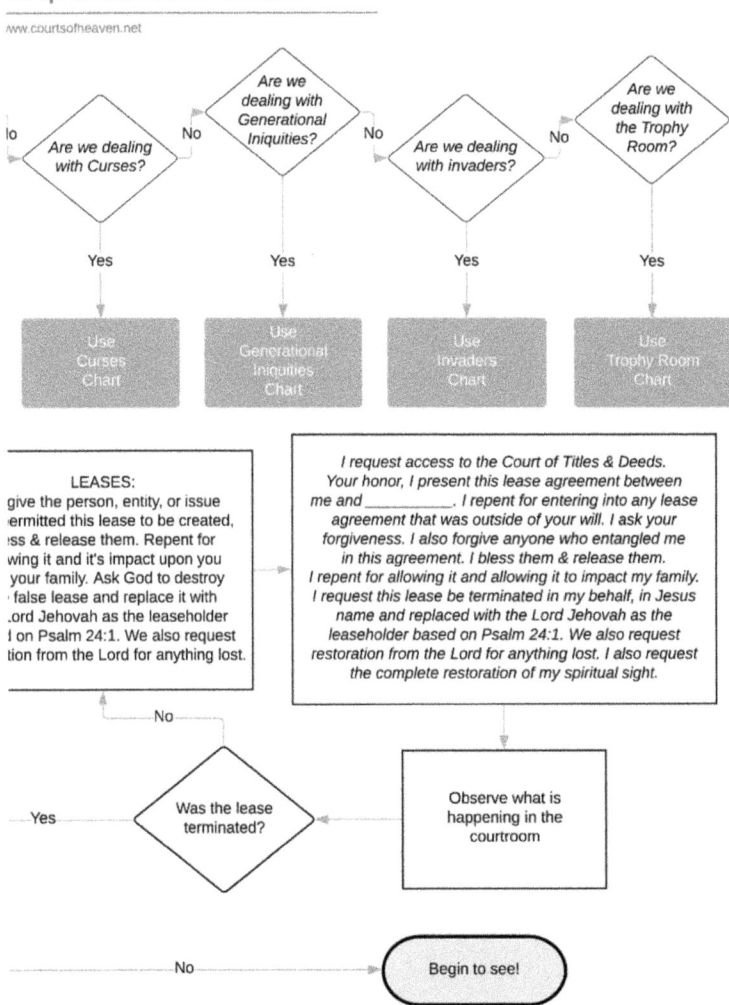

...rship Claims Chart - Leases

www.courtsofheaven.net

```
                    ┌─────────────┐          ┌─────────────┐          ┌─────────────┐          ┌─────────────┐
                    │  Are we     │          │  Are we     │          │  Are we     │          │  Are we     │
          ──No──────│  dealing    │───No─────│  dealing    │───No─────│  dealing    │───No─────│  dealing    │
                    │  with       │          │  with Gen.  │          │  with       │          │  with the   │
                    │  Curses?    │          │  Iniquities?│          │  invaders?  │          │  Trophy Rm? │
                    └──────┬──────┘          └──────┬──────┘          └──────┬──────┘          └──────┬──────┘
                          Yes                      Yes                      Yes                      Yes
                           │                        │                        │                        │
                     ┌─────▼─────┐            ┌─────▼─────┐            ┌─────▼─────┐            ┌─────▼─────┐
                     │   Use     │            │   Use     │            │   Use     │            │   Use     │
                     │  Curses   │            │Generational│           │ Invaders  │            │Trophy Room│
                     │  Chart    │            │ Iniquities │           │  Chart    │            │  Chart    │
                     │           │            │  Chart    │            │           │            │           │
                     └───────────┘            └───────────┘            └───────────┘            └───────────┘
```

LEASES:
...give the person, entity, or issue ...ermitted this lease to be created, ...ss & release them. Repent for ...wing it and it's impact upon you ...your family. Ask God to destroy ...false lease and replace it with ...ord Jehovah as the leaseholder ...d on Psalm 24:1. We also request ...tion from the Lord for anything lost.

→

I request access to the Court of Titles & Deeds. Your honor, I present this lease agreement between me and _____. I repent for entering into any lease agreement that was outside of your will. I ask your forgiveness. I also forgive anyone who entangled me in this agreement. I bless them & release them. I repent for allowing it and allowing it to impact my family. I request this lease be terminated in my behalf, in Jesus name and replaced with the Lord Jehovah as the leaseholder based on Psalm 24:1. We also request restoration from the Lord for anything lost. I also request the complete restoration of my spiritual sight.

◇ Was the lease terminated?
— Yes →
— No → Observe what is happening in the courtroom
— No → **Begin to see!**

None of the processes offered here constitute medical or legal advice. The focus is spiritual direction.

XXVII

Obstacles to See

Dr. Ron M. Horner - w

- Are we dealing with accusations today? — **Yes** → Use Accusations Chart
- Are we dealing with false verdicts? — **Yes** → Use False Verdicts Chart
- Are we dealing with covenants or oaths? — **Yes** → Use Covenants or Oaths Chart
- Are we dealing with Ownership Claims? — **Yes** → Use Ownership Claims Chart

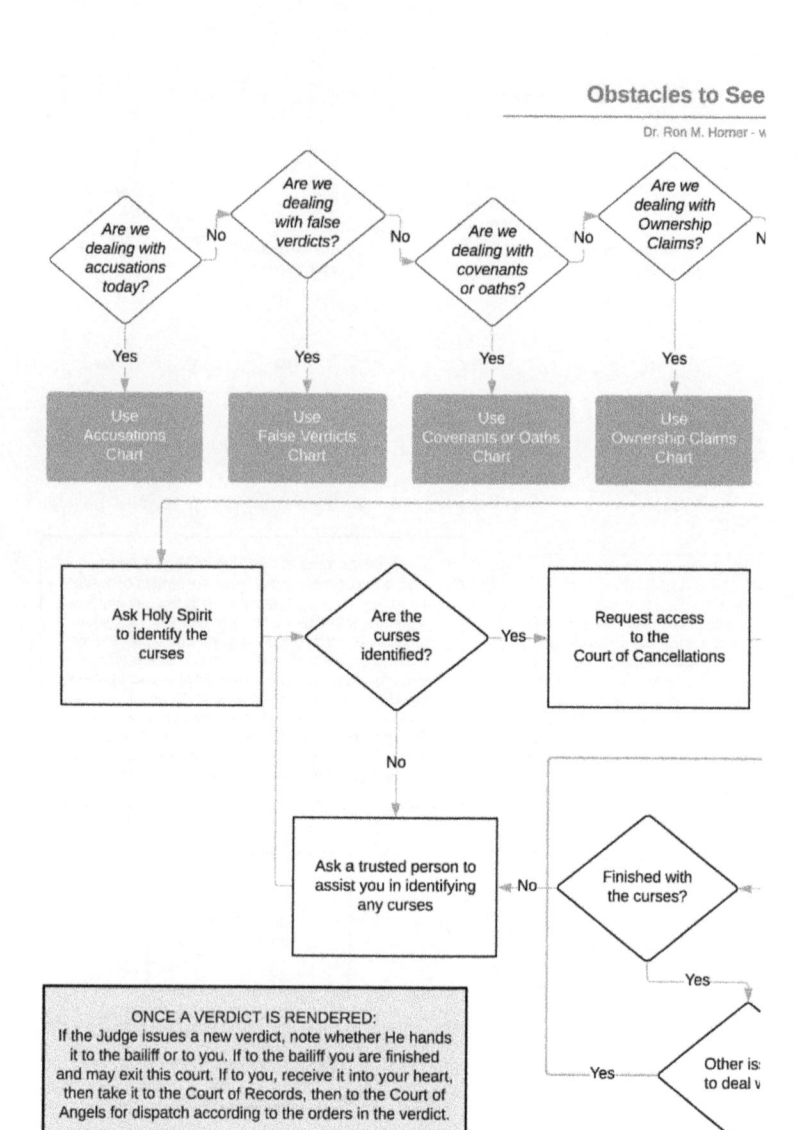

(Each "No" continues to the next question)

Ask Holy Spirit to identify the curses → Are the curses identified?
- **Yes** → Request access to the Court of Cancellations
- **No** → Ask a trusted person to assist you in identifying any curses → Finished with the curses?
  - **Yes** → Other is: to deal v
  - **No** → (loop back)

ONCE A VERDICT IS RENDERED:
If the Judge issues a new verdict, note whether He hands it to the bailiff or to you. If to the bailiff you are finished and may exit this court. If to you, receive it into your heart, then take it to the Court of Records, then to the Court of Angels for dispatch according to the orders in the verdict.

Copyright ©2019 Dr. Ron M. Horner | www.courtsofheaven.net | Use by permission

ing - Curses Chart

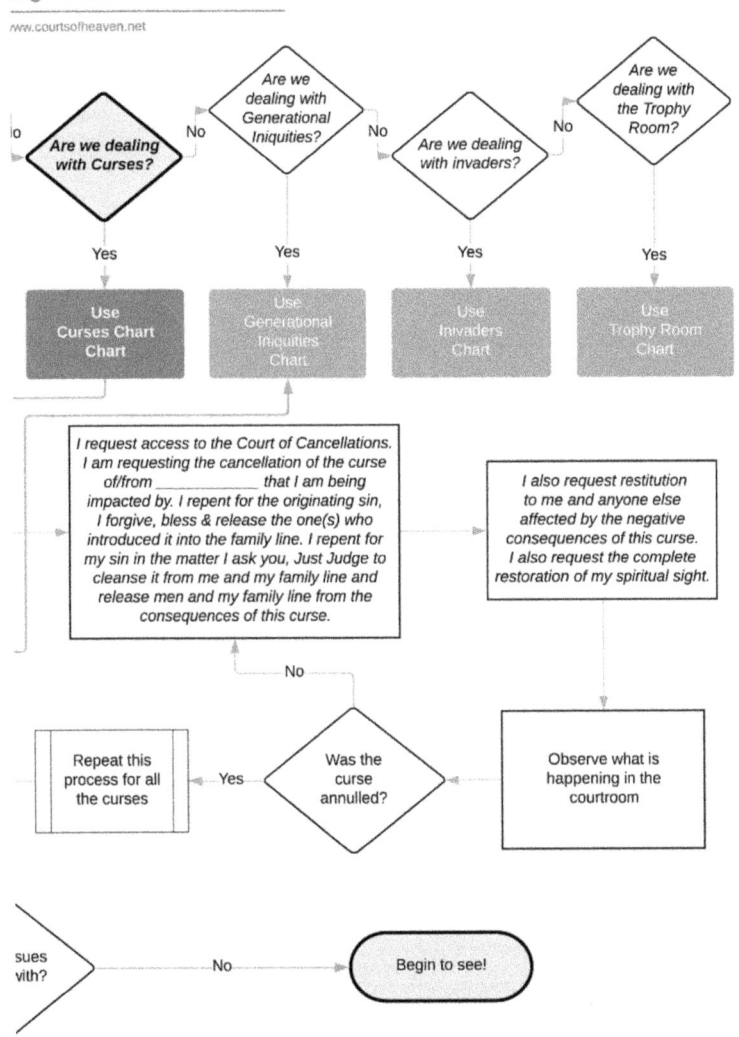

www.courtsofheaven.net

- **Are we dealing with Curses?** → Yes → **Use Curses Chart Chart**
- No → **Are we dealing with Generational Iniquities?** → Yes → **Use Generational Iniquities Chart**
- No → **Are we dealing with invaders?** → Yes → **Use Invaders Chart**
- No → **Are we dealing with the Trophy Room?** → Yes → **Use Trophy Room Chart**

I request access to the Court of Cancellations. I am requesting the cancellation of the curse of/from _____ that I am being impacted by. I repent for the originating sin, I forgive, bless & release the one(s) who introduced it into the family line. I repent for my sin in the matter I ask you, Just Judge to cleanse it from me and my family line and release men and my family line from the consequences of this curse.

I also request restitution to me and anyone else affected by the negative consequences of this curse. I also request the complete restoration of my spiritual sight.

Was the curse annulled?
- Yes → Repeat this process for all the curses
- No → Observe what is happening in the courtroom

sues with? — No → **Begin to see!**

None of the processes offered here constitute medical or legal advice. The focus is spiritual direction.

XXIX

Obstacles to Seeing - Ge[neral]

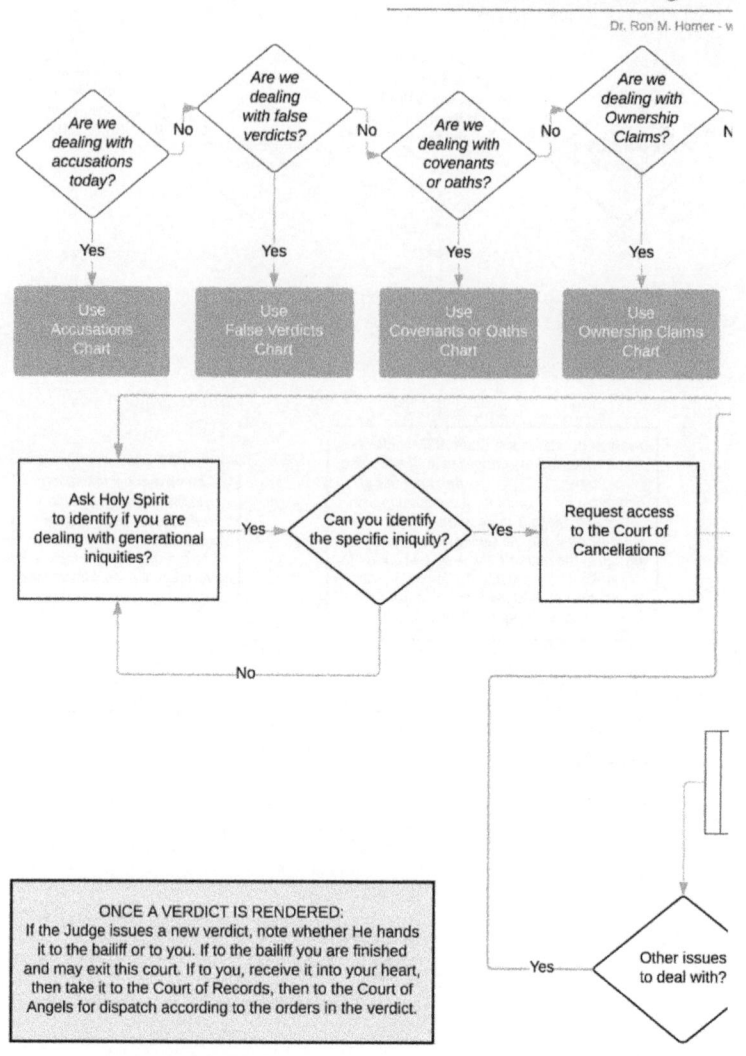

Dr. Ron M. Horner

```
                Are we                  Are we                                Are we
                dealing                 dealing                                dealing with
Are we          with false              with                                   Ownership
dealing with    verdicts?     No        covenants        No                    Claims?      N
accusations                             or oaths?
today?
```

- Yes → Use Accusations Chart
- Yes → Use False Verdicts Chart
- Yes → Use Covenants or Oaths Chart
- Yes → Use Ownership Claims Chart

Ask Holy Spirit to identify if you are dealing with generational iniquities? — Yes → Can you identify the specific iniquity? — Yes → Request access to the Court of Cancellations

No (loops back)

ONCE A VERDICT IS RENDERED:
If the Judge issues a new verdict, note whether He hands it to the bailiff or to you. If to the bailiff you are finished and may exit this court. If to you, receive it into your heart, then take it to the Court of Records, then to the Court of Angels for dispatch according to the orders in the verdict.

Yes → Other issues to deal with?

Copyright ©2019 Dr. Ron M. Horner | www.courtsofheaven.net | Use by permission

xxx

Generational Iniquities Chart

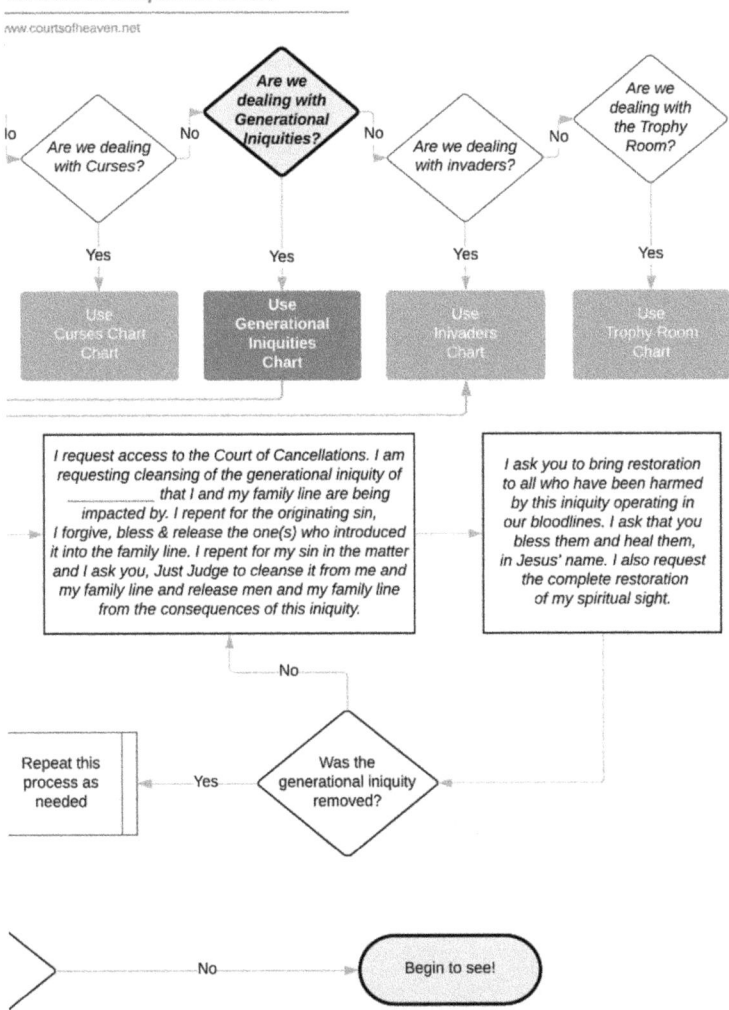

www.courtsofheaven.net

```
                    ┌─────────────────┐
                    │  Are we dealing │
                    │  with Generational│
                    │   Iniquities?   │
                    └─────────────────┘
   ┌──────No─────────┘       │       └────No────┐
   ▼                         │                  ▼
┌──────────┐                 │           ┌──────────┐        ┌──────────┐
│ Are we   │                 │           │ Are we   │──No──▶│ Are we   │
│ dealing  │                 │           │ dealing  │        │ dealing  │
│ with     │                 │           │ with     │        │ with the │
│ Curses?  │                 │           │ invaders?│        │ Trophy   │
└──────────┘                 │           └──────────┘        │ Room?    │
     │                       │                │              └──────────┘
    Yes                     Yes              Yes                  Yes
     ▼                       ▼                ▼                    ▼
┌──────────┐         ┌──────────────┐   ┌──────────┐         ┌──────────┐
│   Use    │         │     Use      │   │   Use    │         │   Use    │
│  Curses  │         │ Generational │   │ Invaders │         │  Trophy  │
│  Chart   │         │  Iniquities  │   │  Chart   │         │   Room   │
│          │         │    Chart     │   │          │         │  Chart   │
└──────────┘         └──────────────┘   └──────────┘         └──────────┘
```

> *I request access to the Court of Cancellations. I am requesting cleansing of the generational iniquity of _____ that I and my family line are being impacted by. I repent for the originating sin, I forgive, bless & release the one(s) who introduced it into the family line. I repent for my sin in the matter and I ask you, Just Judge to cleanse it from me and my family line and release men and my family line from the consequences of this iniquity.*

> *I ask you to bring restoration to all who have been harmed by this iniquity operating in our bloodlines. I ask that you bless them and heal them, in Jesus' name. I also request the complete restoration of my spiritual sight.*

┌──────────────┐   ┌──────────────┐
│ Repeat this │◀──── Yes ─────────│   Was the   │
│ process as │   │ generational │
│   needed   │   │   iniquity   │
└──────────────┘   │   removed?   │
                                    └──────────────┘
                                           │
                                          No
                                           ▼
                                    ┌──────────────┐
                                    │ Begin to see!│
                                    └──────────────┘

None of the processes offered here constitute medical or legal advice. The focus is spiritual direction.

XXXI

Obstacles to Seei[ng]

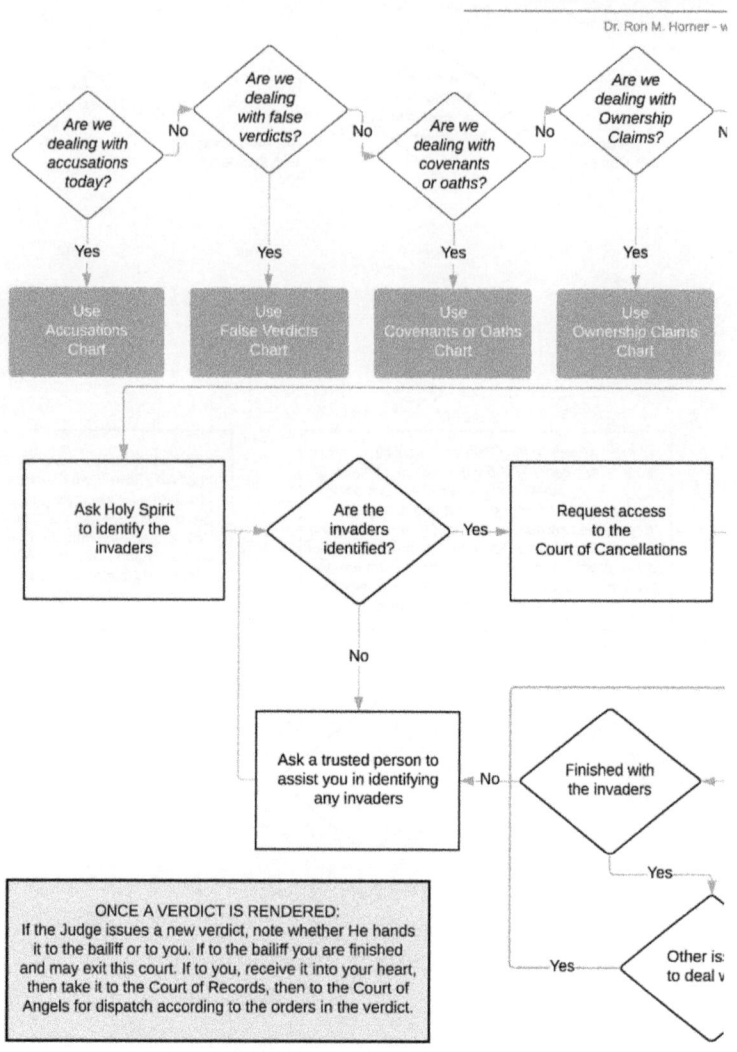

Dr. Ron M. Horner - w

```
                                                                                  
   ┌──────────┐       ┌──────────┐       ┌──────────┐       ┌──────────┐          
   │  Are we  │       │  Are we  │       │          │       │  Are we  │          
   │ dealing  │       │ dealing  │       │  Are we  │       │ dealing  │          
   │   with   │──No──▶│with false│──No──▶│ dealing  │──No──▶│   with   │──N       
   │accusations│      │ verdicts?│       │   with   │       │ Ownership│          
   │  today?  │       │          │       │ covenants│       │  Claims? │          
   └─────┬────┘       └─────┬────┘       │or oaths? │       └─────┬────┘          
        Yes                Yes           └─────┬────┘            Yes              
         ▼                  ▼                 Yes                ▼                
   ┌──────────┐       ┌──────────┐             ▼           ┌──────────┐           
   │   Use    │       │   Use    │       ┌──────────┐      │   Use    │           
   │Accusations│      │False     │       │   Use    │      │Ownership │           
   │  Chart   │       │Verdicts  │       │Covenants │      │Claims    │           
   └──────────┘       │  Chart   │       │or Oaths  │      │Chart     │           
                      └──────────┘       │  Chart   │      └──────────┘           
                                         └──────────┘                             
```

- Ask Holy Spirit to identify the invaders
- Are the invaders identified? — Yes → Request access to the Court of Cancellations
- No ↓
- Ask a trusted person to assist you in identifying any invaders — No → Finished with the invaders
- Yes → Other is: to deal v

ONCE A VERDICT IS RENDERED:
If the Judge issues a new verdict, note whether He hands it to the bailiff or to you. If to the bailiff you are finished and may exit this court. If to you, receive it into your heart, then take it to the Court of Records, then to the Court of Angels for dispatch according to the orders in the verdict.

Copyright ©2019 Dr. Ron M. Horner | www.courtsofheaven.net | Use by permission

ng - Invaders Chart

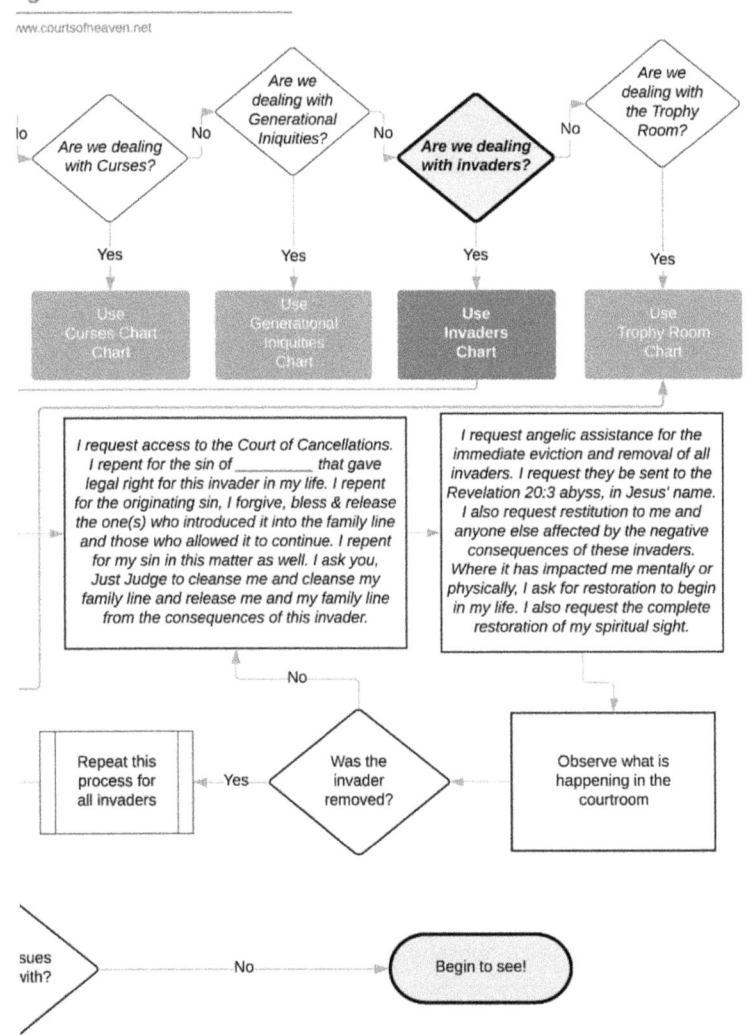

www.courtsofheaven.net

```
                    Are we                    Are we
                  dealing with              dealing with
  Are we    No   Generational   No  Are we dealing  No  the Trophy  No
dealing with      Iniquities?       with invaders?     Room?
  Curses?
    |                 |                 |                 |
   Yes               Yes               Yes               Yes
    ↓                 ↓                 ↓                 ↓
   Use               Use               Use               Use
 Curses Chart   Generational       Invaders         Trophy Room
                 Iniquities          Chart             Chart
                   Chart
```

I request access to the Court of Cancellations. I repent for the sin of _____ that gave legal right for this invader in my life. I repent for the originating sin, I forgive, bless & release the one(s) who introduced it into the family line and those who allowed it to continue. I repent for my sin in this matter as well. I ask you, Just Judge to cleanse me and cleanse my family line and release me and my family line from the consequences of this invader.

I request angelic assistance for the immediate eviction and removal of all invaders. I request they be sent to the Revelation 20:3 abyss, in Jesus' name. I also request restitution to me and anyone else affected by the negative consequences of these invaders. Where it has impacted me mentally or physically, I ask for restoration to begin in my life. I also request the complete restoration of my spiritual sight.

Repeat this process for all invaders ←Yes— Was the invader removed? →No→ Observe what is happening in the courtroom

sues vith? —No— **Begin to see!**

None of the processes offered here constitute medical or legal advice. The focus is spiritual direction.

XXXIII

Obstacles to Seeing

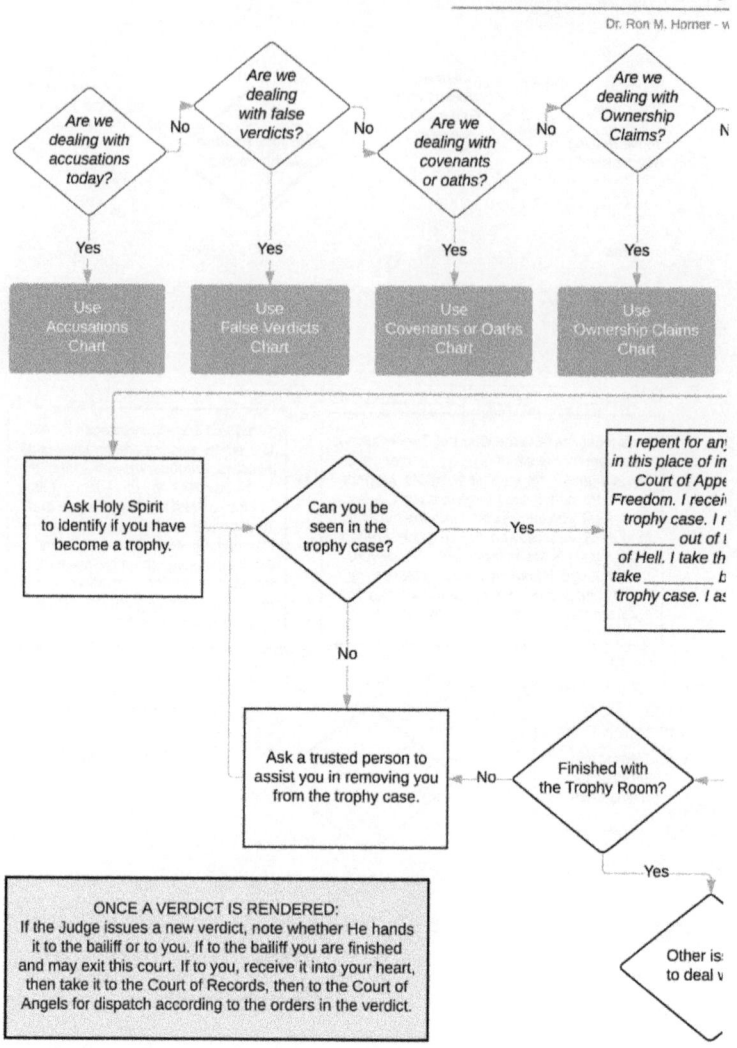

Dr. Ron M. Horner - w

- **Are we dealing with accusations today?** — Yes → Use Accusations Chart / No →
- **Are we dealing with false verdicts?** — Yes → Use False Verdicts Chart / No →
- **Are we dealing with covenants or oaths?** — Yes → Use Covenants or Oaths Chart / No →
- **Are we dealing with Ownership Claims?** — Yes → Use Ownership Claims Chart / N...

Ask Holy Spirit to identify if you have become a trophy. → Can you be seen in the trophy case?

- Yes → I repent for any... in this place of in... Court of Appe... Freedom. I recei... trophy case. I r... _____ out of ... of Hell. I take th... take _____ b... trophy case. I a...
- No → Ask a trusted person to assist you in removing you from the trophy case. → Finished with the Trophy Room? — No (loop back) / Yes → Other is... to deal v...

ONCE A VERDICT IS RENDERED:
If the Judge issues a new verdict, note whether He hands it to the bailiff or to you. If to the bailiff you are finished and may exit this court. If to you, receive it into your heart, then take it to the Court of Records, then to the Court of Angels for dispatch according to the orders in the verdict.

Copyright ©2019 Dr. Ron M. Horner | www.courtsofheaven.net | Use by permission

- Trophy Room Chart

www.courtsofheaven.net

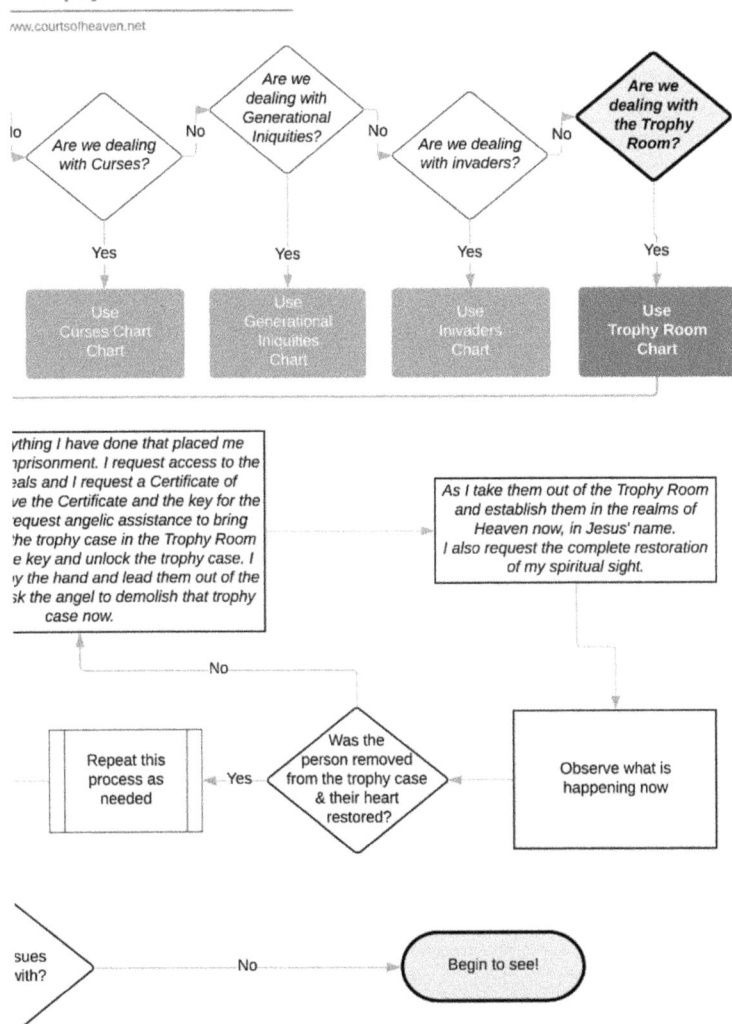

```
                    ┌─────────────┐         ┌─────────────┐         ┌─────────────┐         ┌─────────────┐
                    │  Are we     │         │  Are we     │         │             │         │  Are we     │
                    │  dealing    │   No    │  dealing    │   No    │  Are we     │   No    │  dealing    │
               ◇────│  with       │────────▶│  with       │────────▶│  dealing    │────────▶│  with       │
                    │  Curses?    │         │ Generational│         │  with       │         │  the Trophy │
                    │             │         │ Iniquities? │         │  invaders?  │         │  Room?      │
                    └──────┬──────┘         └──────┬──────┘         └──────┬──────┘         └──────┬──────┘
                           │ Yes                   │ Yes                   │ Yes                   │ Yes
                           ▼                       ▼                       ▼                       ▼
                    ┌─────────────┐         ┌─────────────┐         ┌─────────────┐         ┌─────────────┐
                    │     Use     │         │     Use     │         │     Use     │         │     Use     │
                    │ Curses Chart│         │ Generational│         │  Invaders   │         │ Trophy Room │
                    │    Chart    │         │  Iniquities │         │    Chart    │         │    Chart    │
                    │             │         │    Chart    │         │             │         │             │
                    └─────────────┘         └─────────────┘         └─────────────┘         └──────┬──────┘
```

...ything I have done that placed me
...prisonment. I request access to the
...als and I request a Certificate of
...ve the Certificate and the key for the
...equest angelic assistance to bring
...he trophy case in the Trophy Room
...e key and unlock the trophy case. I
...y the hand and lead them out of the
...k the angel to demolish that trophy
case now.

As I take them out of the Trophy Room
and establish them in the realms of
Heaven now, in Jesus' name.
I also request the complete restoration
of my spiritual sight.

┌─────────────┐   ┌─────────────┐   ┌─────────────┐
│ Repeat this│   │ Was the   │   │ Observe what│
│ process as │◀── Yes ──│ person removed│──────▶│ is happening│
│   needed   │   │ from the trophy case│ │   now   │
└─────────────┘   │ & their heart│   └─────────────┘
                         │ restored? │
                         └─────────────┘

sues
vith? ─────── No ──────▶ (Begin to see!)

None of the processes offered here constitute medical or legal advice. The focus is spiritual direction.

Obstacles to Seeing - R[...]

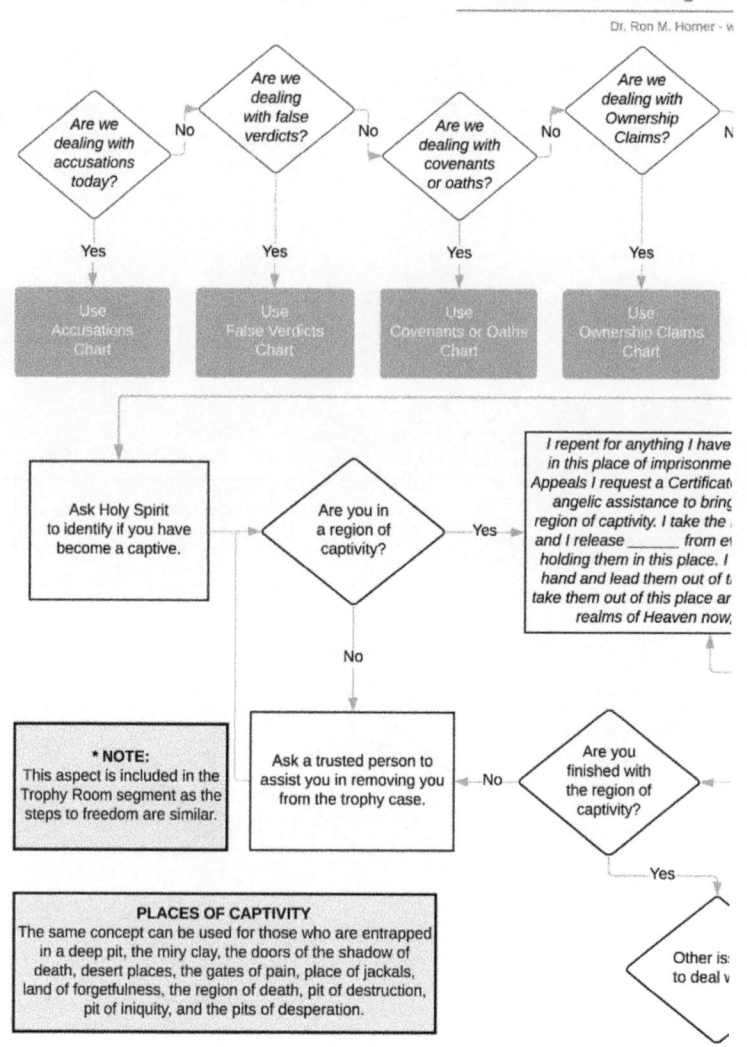

Dr. Ron M. Horner - w[...]

- Are we dealing with accusations today? — **No** → Are we dealing with false verdicts? — **No** → Are we dealing with covenants or oaths? — **No** → Are we dealing with Ownership Claims? — N[...]
  - **Yes** ↓ Use Accusations Chart
  - **Yes** ↓ Use False Verdicts Chart
  - **Yes** ↓ Use Covenants or Oaths Chart
  - **Yes** ↓ Use Ownership Claims Chart

Ask Holy Spirit to identify if you have become a captive. → Are you in a region of captivity? — **Yes** → I repent for anything I have [...] in this place of imprisonme[...] Appeals I request a Certificat[...] angelic assistance to bring [...] region of captivity. I take the [...] and I release _____ from ev[...] holding them in this place. I [...] hand and lead them out of t[...] take them out of this place a[...] realms of Heaven now,

No ↓

Ask a trusted person to assist you in removing you from the trophy case. — **No** → Are you finished with the region of captivity?

* NOTE: This aspect is included in the Trophy Room segment as the steps to freedom are similar.

Yes →

Other is[...] to deal [...]

PLACES OF CAPTIVITY
The same concept can be used for those who are entrapped in a deep pit, the miry clay, the doors of the shadow of death, desert places, the gates of pain, place of jackals, land of forgetfulness, the region of death, pit of destruction, pit of iniquity, and the pits of desperation.

Copyright ©2019 Dr. Ron M. Horner | www.courtsofheaven.net | Use by permission

Regions of Captivity Chart

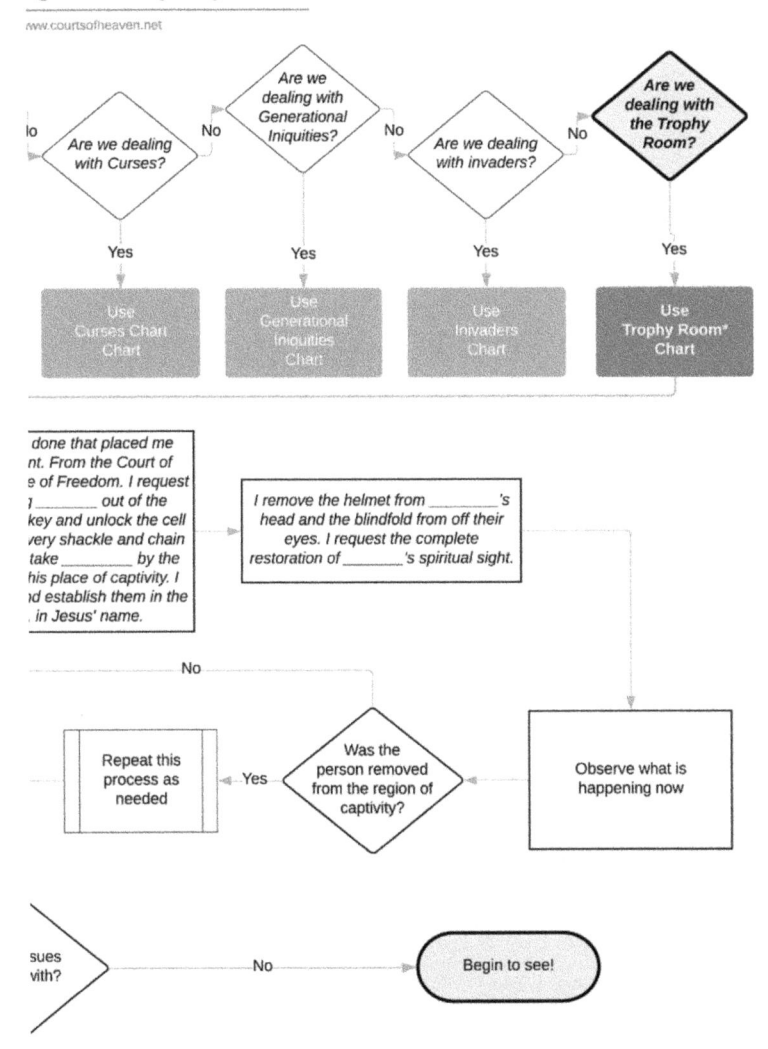

www.courtsofheaven.net

```
         ┌─────────────┐        ┌─────────────┐        ┌─────────────┐        ┌─────────────┐
         │   Are we    │  No    │   Are we    │  No    │   Are we    │  No    │   Are we    │
   ──→   │ dealing with│ ────→  │ dealing with│ ────→  │ dealing with│ ────→  │ dealing with│
         │   Curses?   │        │ Generational│        │  invaders?  │        │ the Trophy  │
         │             │        │ Iniquities? │        │             │        │    Room?    │
         └──────┬──────┘        └──────┬──────┘        └──────┬──────┘        └──────┬──────┘
                │ Yes                  │ Yes                  │ Yes                  │ Yes
                ▼                      ▼                      ▼                      ▼
         ┌─────────────┐        ┌─────────────┐        ┌─────────────┐        ┌─────────────┐
         │     Use     │        │     Use     │        │     Use     │        │     Use     │
         │ Curses Chart│        │ Generational│        │   Invaders  │        │ Trophy Room │
         │             │        │  Iniquities │        │    Chart    │        │    Chart    │
         │             │        │    Chart    │        │             │        │             │
         └─────────────┘        └─────────────┘        └─────────────┘        └─────────────┘
```

... done that placed me ... nt. From the Court of ... e of Freedom. I request ... _____ out of the key and unlock the cell very shackle and chain take _____ by the his place of captivity. I ... establish them in the ... in Jesus' name.

I remove the helmet from _____'s head and the blindfold from off their eyes. I request the complete restoration of _____'s spiritual sight.

——— No ———

| Repeat this process as needed | ←— Yes — | Was the person removed from the region of captivity? | ——— | Observe what is happening now |

... sues ... with? ——— No ——— → **Begin to see!**

None of the processes offered here constitute medical or legal advice. The focus is spiritual direction.

XXXVII

Obstacles to Seeing

Dr. Ron M. Horner - www

```
Are we dealing with accusations today?  --No-->  Are we dealing with false verdicts?  --No-->  Are we dealing with covenants or oaths?  --No-->  Are we dealing with Ownership Claims?  --No-->
        |                                                |                                          |                                                 |
       Yes                                              Yes                                        Yes                                               Yes
        ↓                                                ↓                                          ↓                                                 ↓
   Use Accusations Chart                         Use False Verdicts Chart              Use Covenants or Oaths Chart                       Use Ownership Claims Chart
```

Recall the last time you could see clearly & invite Jesus into the scene → Is Jesus with you in the scene? —Yes→ Allow the fear to dissipate

No
↓
Ask a trusted person to assist you in revisiting the situation. ←—No—

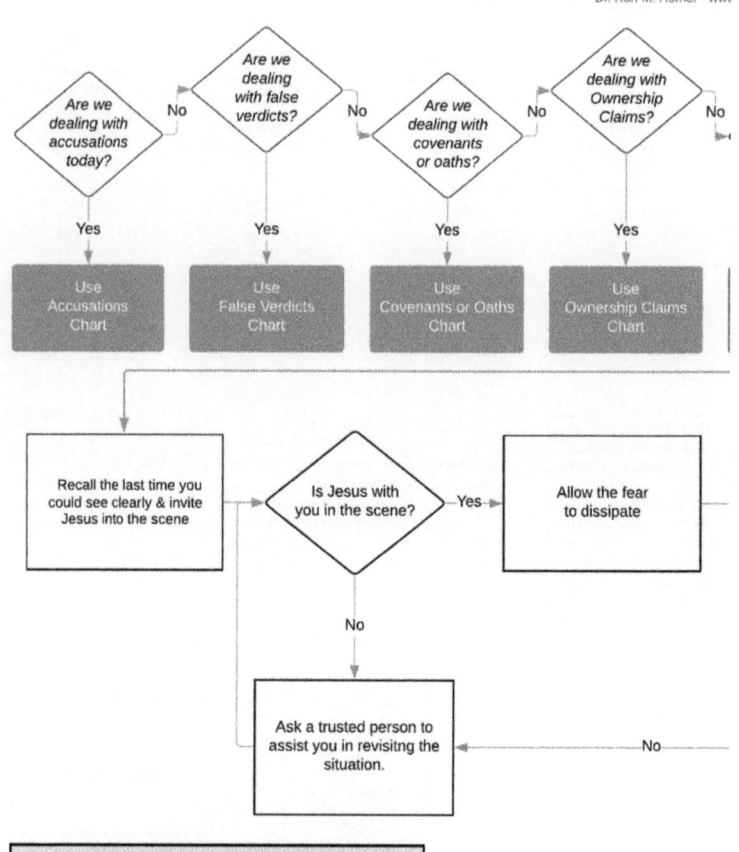

ONCE A VERDICT IS RENDERED:
If the Judge issues a new verdict, note whether He hands it to the bailiff or to you. If to the bailiff you are finished and may exit this court. If to you, receive it into your heart, then take it to the Court of Records, then to the Court of Angels for dispatch according to the orders in the verdict.

Copyright ©2019 Dr. Ron M. Horner | www.courtsofheaven.net | Use by permission

1g - Release from Fear

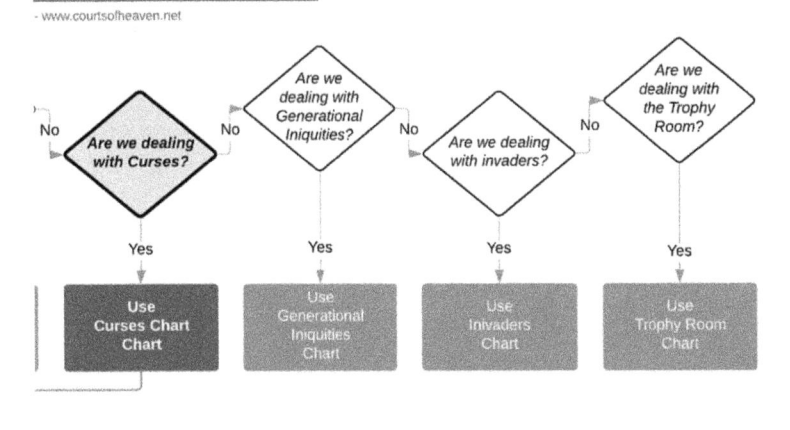

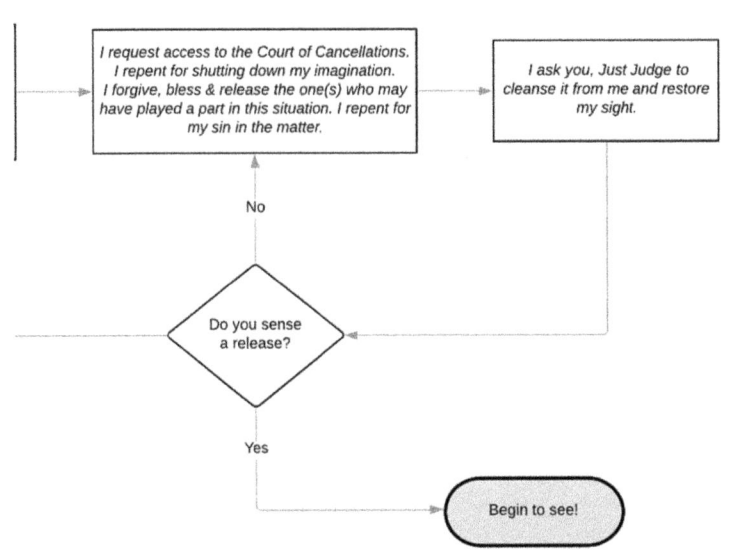

- www.courtsofheaven.net

Are we dealing with Curses? — No → ... / Yes → **Use Curses Chart Chart**

Are we dealing with Generational Iniquities? — No → / Yes → **Use Generational Iniquities Chart**

Are we dealing with invaders? — No → / Yes → **Use Invaders Chart**

Are we dealing with the Trophy Room? — No → / Yes → **Use Trophy Room Chart**

> I request access to the Court of Cancellations. I repent for shutting down my imagination. I forgive, bless & release the one(s) who may have played a part in this situation. I repent for my sin in the matter.

> I ask you, Just Judge to cleanse it from me and restore my sight.

Do you sense a release?
- No → (loop back)
- Yes → **Begin to see!**

None of the processes offered here constitute medical or legal advice. The focus is spiritual direction.

XXXIX

Description

Removing the Blockages to Spiritual Sight

Do you have trouble seeing in the realm of the Spirit? If you do, I have some solutions for you. In our work in the Courts of Heaven, we discovered keys to unlock your spiritual seeing abilities. We have excellent results from these keys. Don't continue in spiritual blindness or being unable to see clearly or consistently. These keys will help you unlock your spiritual seeing today!

Works Cited

American Heritage Dictionary of the English Language, Fifth Edition. (2016). Houghton Mifflin Harcourt Publishing Company.

Moffatt, J. A. (1994). *The Bible: James Moffatt Translation.* Grand Rapids: Kregel Publications.

Strong, J. (1890). *The Exhaustive Concordance of the Bible.* Cincinnati: Jennings & Graham.

Tolman, K. (2017). *Moved with Compassion.* Portland: Restoration Gateway Ministries.

Unknown. (2019, January 5). *Freedictionary.com/banz.* Retrieved from Freedictionary.com: https://www.thefreedictionary.com/Bann

Virkler, D. M. (Director). (2018). *Hearing God Through Your Dreams – Session 1 – Bridges to the Supernatural, Charity Kayembe* [Motion Picture].

Book Summary

ENGAGING THE COURTS SERIES

Engaging the Mercy Court of Heaven

Embracing an Additional Paradigm of Prayer

In Luke 18, Jesus subtly introduces the third paradigm of prayer. The courtroom paradigm has gone overlooked throughout church history. Only in the last few years has this truth been uncovered with amazing results. Prayers that have long gone unanswered are answered in a matter of days or even hours. Situations from which no hope seemed available are turning around.

The Courts of Heaven paradigm is available to every believer. It will help thrust efforts of intercession into new levels of breakthrough. Once every legal obstacle hindering the answer to your prayers is removed, the answers will come. As we learn to engage the Courts of Heaven, lives will change – your life will change. You will experience answered prayer on a level you may have not thought possible.

Engaging the Mercy Court is the introductory book to the Courts of Heaven prayer paradigm.

Available in Paperback, Spiral, Kindle, & PDF.

Also available in Spanish & Afrikaans (240 pages)

——— · ———

Engaging the Courts of Healing & the Healing Gardens

Embracing a New Paradigm of Healing

God has wonderfully provided for our healing and health via the Courts of Healing and the Healing Garden. Join with us as we explore this amazing complex designed to help you experience the riches of God's goodness and see the Apostle John's prayer manifested in your life:

Beloved, I wish above all things that you would prosper and be in health even as your soul prospers. (3 John 2)

Learn the obstacles to healing and how to get them removed, discover how to intercede for others and see lives changed. No sickness, disease, or condition is beyond the scope of God's provision in the Courts of Healing, Heaven's Hospital and the Healing Garden. May you experience God's healing in your life.

Available in Paperback, Spiral, Kindle, & PDF (250 pages)

——— · ———

Engaging the Courts of Heaven

Just how many Courts are there?

This book explores over a dozen of the Courts of Heaven with which I have had experience. Not for the novice, but for the seasoned veteran of the Courts of Heaven. It also covers how to establish an ecclesia in your region for permanent transformation.

Available in Paperback, Spiral, Kindle, & PDF (232 pages)

―――― · ――――

Engaging the Courts for Ownership & Order

Have you ever felt owned?

Many things can attempt to "own" us — emotions, medical diagnoses, family traits, and more! Let this book help you explore freedom in ways you have not even imagined.

Available in Paperback, Spiral, Kindle, & PDF (162 pages)

―――― · ――――

Engaging the Help Desk
of the Courts of Heaven

Ever need help in the Courts?

God has wondrously provided assistance in the Courts of Heaven. Don't know where to go? Ask the Help Desk. Don't know what to do? Ask the Help Desk. It is amazing what awaits us in the Courts of Heaven.

Available in Paperback, Kindle, & PDF (102 pages)

——— · ———

Engaging the Courts
for Decrees from Heaven

Receiving God's Stamp of Approval

Do we want Heaven to move when we decree? Then we must follow the protocol of the Court of Decrees within the Courts of Heaven. Heaven has a protocol for seeing decrees fully manifest on the earth. Decrees with the approval of Heaven, change the earth permanently!

Available in Paperback, Kindle, & PDF (154 pages)

——— · ———

Engaging the Courts of Healing and the Healing Gardens

Embracing a New Paradigm for Healing

God has wonderfully provided for our healing and health via the Courts of Healing and the Healing Garden. Join with us as we explore this amazing complex designed to help you experience the riches of God's goodness and see the Apostle John's prayer manifested in your life:

Beloved, I wish above all things that you would prosper and be in health even as your soul prospers. (3 John 2)

Learn the obstacles to healing and how to get them removed, discover how to intercede for others, and see lives changed. No sickness, disease, or condition is beyond the scope of God's provision in the Courts of Healing, Heaven's Hospital and the Healing Garden. May you experience God's healing in your life.

Available in Paperback, Spiral, & PDF

———·———

Engaging the Courts for Your City

Building Ecclesias to Enhance the Kingdom

Do you want to impact your city through prayer? Do you need a new paradigm by which to see massive change and see your city transformed?

Leader's Guide and Workbook available.

Available in Paperback, Spiral, & PDF (212 pages)

──── · ────

Engaging the Courts for Your City Leader's Guide

Do you want to impact your city through prayer? Do you need a new paradigm by which to see massive change and see your city transformed?

PowerPoint Presentation included.
Workbook also available.

Available in Paperback, Spiral, & PDF (152 pages)

──── · ────

L

Engaging the Courts for Your City Workbook

Do you want to impact your city through prayer? Do you need a new paradigm by which to see massive change and see your city transformed?

Available in Paperback & PDF (46 pages)

——— · ———

Four Keys to Defeating Accusations

Dismantle the Accusations
that are Destroying Your Life

Accusations have great power to destroy your life and must be dealt with before they do. They create cases against you in the Courts of Heaven. An accusation aims to divert you from your destiny. Accusations seek to define you and limit you and wear you down. Dismantling accusations is key to effectively fulfilling your purpose and cannot simply be ignored; accusations must be destroyed! Learn how in this book!

Available in Paperback, Kindle, & PDF (68 pages)

——— · ———

Adoptando Un Paradigma Adicional de Oración

En Lucas 18, Jesús introduce sutilmente un tercer paradigma de oración. El paradigma del juzgado ha pasado inadvertido a través de la historia de la iglesia. Esta verdad no fue descubierta hasta hace algunos años, con resultados asombrosos. Oraciones que han quedado sin respuesta por mucho tiempo han sido respondidas en cuestión de días o incluso horas. Situaciones sin esperanza aparente han dado un vuelco.

Esta verdad es para todos los creyentes, pero también llevará a los esfuerzos de intercesión a nuevos niveles al acceder a la Corte Celestial de Misericordia.Una vez que sea removido todo obstáculo legal que impide la respuesta a tusoraciones, estas serán respondidas. A medida que aprendemos a proceder en las Cortes del Cielo, las vidas cambiarán – tu vida cambiará. Experimentarás el ver tus oraciones respondidas a un nivel como nunca creíste posible.

Aferra estas verdades y empieza a interactuar con las Cortes del Cielo. La Corte entra en sesión... ¡todos de pie!

Available in Paperback, Spiral, Kindle, & PDF (196 pages)

OVERCOMING SERIES

Overcoming Verdicts from the Courts of Hell

Releasing False Verdicts

Have you found yourself struggling with situations or mindsets from which you could find no relief? We have not yet awakened to the fact that we may have been facing a false judgment arising out of the Courts of Hell.

Available in Paperback, Kindle, & PDF (140 pages)

——— · ———

Overcoming the False Verdicts of Freemasonry

Are you free from Freemasonry?

In all the materials I have seen on freedom from freemasonry, none has ever dealt with the false verdicts that empower the various levels of Freemasonry. This book does! Find freedom! Begin today!

Available in Paperback, Spiral, Kindle, & PDF (308 pages)

——— · ———

ENGAGING HEAVEN SERIES

Cooperating with The Glory

Learning a New Way of Ministering

Scripture promises that the earth will be filled with the knowledge of the Glory of the Lord as the waters cover the sea. To accomplish that goal, God will use willing saints—men and women who desire to see God move and are wise enough to allow Him to move as He desires.

As we learn to release Heaven on the earth, we will experience societal change. However, God will start with the church and your home to release His Glory into first. Learn how to cooperate with Heaven in release The Glory. Lives will change, and YOU will never be the same!

Available in Paperback, Kindle, & PDF (136 pages)

———·———

OTHER BOOKS

Divorced!

Obtaining Freedom
from the Sun and Moon God

Written by Jeanette Strauss & Doug Carr, Edited by Dr. Ron M. Horner

The Body of Christ has been facing an enemy that it has little knowledge or understanding of, much less how to overcome this insidious foe – the principality of Baal, the sun god, and his counterpart Allah – the moon god. We must divorce these principalities from our lives to make the necessary progress in our daily lives.

The strategy to gain the victory over these principalities is through Courts of Heaven intercession. We will obtain the legal right through repentance and forgiveness for sin committed against God to remove the lawful rights Baal and Allah has used to withhold from us and our families, churches, businesses, cities, towns, and regions. This series of petitions of divorce are geared for individual, family, church or ministry, businesses, or regions or territories. Utilize these petitions to gain the freedom purchased by the blood of Jesus Christ.

Available in Paperback, Spiral, Kindle, & PDF (196 pages)